Manor Gardens Centre
1913-2013

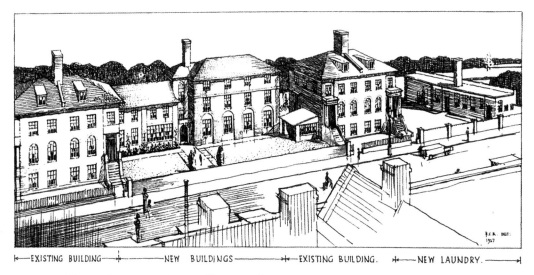

|←—EXISTING BUILDING—→|————NEW BUILDINGS————→|←—EXISTING BUILDING. —→|←——NEW LAUNDRY.——→|

NORTH ISLINGTON INFANT WELFARE CENTRE. SKETCH SHEWING EXTENSION OF BUILDINGS.

Sketch of 6-7 and 8-9 Manor Gardens with new extensions. Architect Arthur Keen RIBA, 1927.

Published 2013
by Manor Gardens Welfare Trust
6-9 Manor Gardens, Islington, London N7 6LA
admin@manorgardenscentre.org
www.manorgardenscentre.org
Telephone 020 7272 4231

Registered Charity No. 1063053
Registered Company No. 3386929.

ISBN 978-0-9574300-0-6
British Library Cataloguing-in-Publication Data
A catalogue record for this work is available at the British Library

Produced for Manor Gardens Welfare Trust by Historical Publications Ltd
14 Saddleton Road, Whitstable, Kent CT5 4JD
(Tel: 01227 272605)
Text typeset in 10.5 Book Antiqua
Printed in China by South China Printing Company

Manor Gardens Centre
1913-2013

*a century of service
in community health and social care*

Andrew Turton

HISTORICAL PUBLICATIONS LTD

Florence Keen OBE, 1868-1942.

This book is dedicated to all those
who have given freely of their time,
personal resources and loyalty to the
Manor Gardens Centre enterprise
in its first century.

From *Jerusalem* by William Blake
(written 1801-20)

It is better to prevent misery than to release from misery.
It is better to prevent error than to forgive the criminal.
Labour well the minute particulars, attend to the little ones,
And those who are in misery cannot remain so long,
If we do but our duty. Labour well the teeming earth.

He who would do good to another must do it in minute particulars,
'General Good' is the plea of the scoundrel, hypocrite and flatterer.
For art and science cannot exist but in minute particulars,
And not in generalising demonstrations of the rational power.
The infinite alone resides in definite and determinate identity.
(chapter 3 lines 49-53 and 60-64)

The lines highlighted were selected by Florence Keen
to be a motto for the Centre.
They were printed at the head of the Annual Report until 1986.
They were also appreciated by our Royal Patron Queen Elizabeth,
the Queen Mother, who had read them in our Annual Reports.
They were quoted in her first official biography.

This three-dimensional image (58 x 56 cm) of a loosely dressed standing child is in the tyle of the Italian Renaissance Rotondo (Tondo). Its origin is unknown. It was attached to the outside wall of the entrance to the new building in 1928, and removed inside in 2006.

Acknowledgements

My appreciative thanks for their help and support are due to:

Members of the Keen family: Maurice Keen (1933-2012), Patience Bayley, Ursula Carter, Geraldine Norman and Robert Warner, for conversation, sight and copies of family papers, paintings and photographs, and to Charles Keen for permission to use his mother's painting of the Keen family.

Members of the two research teams from the University of the Third Age (North London branches) who conducted 'shared learning projects' in 2006 and 2010. This was a trailblazing effort; particular thanks to Phyllis Rosenberg who convened both projects, and to her late husband Martin Rosenberg.

Past members of the staff, directors and trustees of the Manor Gardens Centre; Jane Lethbridge, Laura MacGillivray, Teresa Bednall, Phyllis Willmott (author of the 75th anniversary booklet), Linda Massie.

Special thanks to Noreen Nicholson and Frank Wood for their careful and critical reading of the manuscript.

Current members of the staff and volunteers at the Manor Gardens Centre, especially: Phillip Watson, Christa Moeckli, Kath Birkett, Chris O'Kane, Hekate Papadaki, William Meghoma, Norma Parsad and John Grice.

All Trustees of the Manor Gardens Welfare Trust with whom I have worked (a list of current Trustees is given in an appendix).

Ann Byrne, CEO, Women's Therapy Centre.

Members of Az Theatre; Jonathan Chadwick, Jonathan Meth and Sheelah Sloane.

Members of various departments of the Borough of Islington, Islington Schools, North Library, Islington Local History Centre and the Islington Museum.

Staff of the London Metropolitan Archives, Highgate Literary and Scientific Institution, the Wellcome Foundation and the British Library.

Robert Aberman for photographs of Manor Gardens Centre since 2000 commissioned by the Centre.

Susan Gooding, Photographer and Manor Gardens web site designer, for photographs taken in 2012 commissiond by the Centre.

John Richardson of Historical Publications Ltd, for sourcing a number of illustrations.

Most illustrations are in the possession of the Manor Garden Centre, others are in the public domain.

My wife Antonia Benedek and daughters Polly and Clio for their love and support, and especially Antonia for her exacting critique of the text.

I take full responsibility for the final version.

Andrew Turton
Upper Holloway, Islington 2013.

Contents

and Aneurin Bevan; Changing of the Guard; Dr Eve Atkins; Alan Fabes ACA; Althea Davis; The rise and decline of mothers and babies clinics; Immigration and a multi-ethnic society; Play and education for under-fives; Governance 1948-77

101 Part Six
RENEWAL AND TRANSFORMATION
Voluntary Action; The Geraldine Aves watershed 1977-80; Dame Geraldine Aves (1898-1986); A major review; Women and the Centre; Governance and management from 1980; Finances and financial management; Services provided from 1977; Two case studies: The Stroke Project and Health Advocacy Project; The Board of Trustees; Practice and strategy 2009-2013; Current situation; Manor Gardens Centre estate; Are we a Community Centre?; the Manor Gardens Centre team; Current needs

134 Part Seven:
REVIEW AND REFLECTIONS
Services then and now; Style and method of work: The Manor Gardens Centre spirit; Training and enablement; Holistic approach; Partnership; Problems of longer term planning

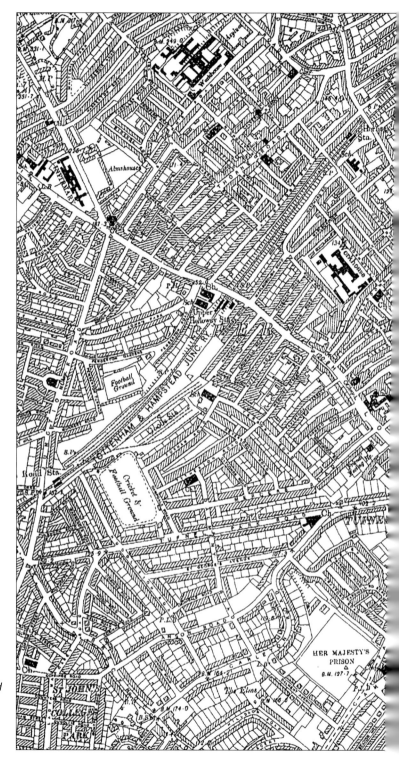

*Map of North Islington, 1894.
Manor Gardens is at the
centre, with a half-mile radius
to Archway and Holloway Road
underground stations. This was
the catchment area for most
Manor Gardens clientele for
many decades.*

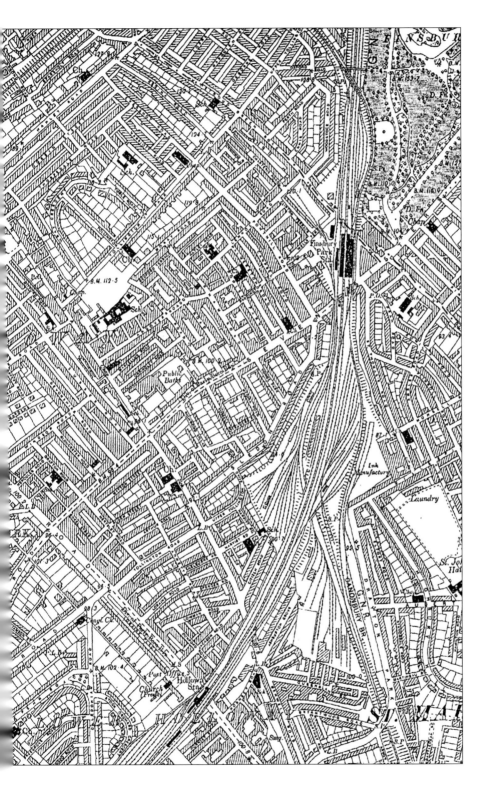

Introduction

I have written this book to mark the Centenary of the Manor Gardens Centre in 2013. It is a record of what has been achieved and how it has been achieved. More than just a record, it is an analytical social history of a charitable institution providing health and welfare services in the community of Islington and some neighbouring areas of North London. It reflects on what did and did not happen, on what could and could not happen. It has much to say about the changing demographics and needs of the local population in changing political contexts of health and welfare provision, and the people who were prominent in leading the team and volunteering their time and cash resources to make things happen.

The book is also a celebration. It marks the centenary with pride in what has been achieved and in the efforts of our forebears to reach such high standards and overcome so many obstacles: recessions, wars, epidemics, lack of funds and the dangers of external controls sapping our independence.

I hope the book may contribute to an understanding of the current situation and our plans, strategies and imaginings for the future. I also hope that it provides insights into the way health and social care delivery has evolved at a local level in a way that we can learn lessons applicable on a wider level for the future.

Our story is a long one. It is a rare example of a multi-purpose health and welfare centre that has remained an independent charity for so long within the 'Third' or 'Voluntary' Sector. It represents a unique twentieth century case study and an opportunity for further study and the learning of lessons for the twenty-first century.

As the book was going to press we learnt that the Heritage Lottery Fund had awarded us £76,000 to initiate the Manor Gardens Community Health Centre. This will collect, create and digitise material on our history and make it available locally and nationally. Ed Bartram has been appointed to the part-time post of Curator.

The history of the Manor Gardens Centre has a significant bearing on the women's movement in the twentieth century, the history of childhood and the history of volunteering. It is also a model of good relations between the voluntary and statutory sectors, public authorities at borough and national levels. A special instance of this is the work of the Centre in the two World Wars that devastated so much in the first half of the last century. Operating on the home front and engaged in Civil Defence, First Aid, Evacuation and Air Raid Warning and

INTRODUCTION

Protection, the Centre showed what an important localised resource such a community organisation can be in time of war or civil emergency.

The structure of the book

The book is written as a single cumulative narrative in approximately chronological order, with some more reflective passages. I hope it will be enjoyable to read it in this way. I have chosen to divide the book into a large number of sections in order to assist readers who may wish to refer to particular periods and issues.

I have attempted to offer balance between the various periods and decades of the history of the Manor Gardens Centre. Thus it is roughly divided between three major periods, each corresponding to a third of the century. These periods are:

1913-1947: building up the Centre, independence and philanthropy, to the end of full-time baby wards;

1948-1979: independence within the NHS, to the end of mother and baby clinics;

1980-2013: from the watershed of Dame Geraldine Ave's chairmanship to the present multifunctional centre.

There are other moments of great importance that subdivide this rather tidy periodisation:

1940-1946: the Second World War and greater reliance on the local authority;

2000-: departure of all NHS services; new significance of the Board of Trustees and the CEO; end of the Keen family involvement.

The book nonetheless may give the feeling of bias towards the early years and the more recent past. The emphasis on the earlier years, the 'era of private philanthropy', and the heritage of this period can be justified by the fact that the generations of the founding figures and their children were preponderant from 1913-1977, nearly two-thirds of our century. This continuity helped to ensure that the purpose, style and spirit of the whole undertaking remained intact and was able to inform and enthuse those who followed. There is also an emphasis on recent years and reflections on the century. The Centre is resolutely looking forward to its second century of service. The book tries to provide a background of information and analysis that may help those who carry this mission forward.

Sources

The book has its limitations. It has not aspired to be a complete or definitive account. There are still sources and archives to be consulted. It is designed to be accessible while conforming to proper standards of roundedness and accuracy. It also had to be produced on time!

A most important source material has been the regular and comprehensive

Annual Reports. These include substantial commentaries on the year's work, schedules of activity, comparative health statistics, lists of donors and audited accounts. Most of the Centre's archive up to about 2000 is kept safely and systematically in the London Metropolitan Archives, which to our good fortune is located in south Islington. At the Centre we have a considerable photographic archive, minutes of various committees, some correspondence, press cuttings and so on. All sources are referenced at the back of the book.

Style: names and titles
I have tried to deal with problems of anachronism and have erred on the side of simplicity and ease of reading. Some of the issues are discussed further in the text.

The Centre
The name of the Centre has undergone several changes, some slight, some more significant. We have come a long way from 'North Islington Infant Welfare Centre and School for Mothers'. The terms 'the Centre' and even just 'Manor Gardens' have long been used in brief, informal reference. We dropped references to locality as we spread our reach. 'School for Mothers' has an archaic ring to it, and the focus of our work over the past thirty years or so has gone well beyond babies and their mothers, though toddlers, young people and families are still very much part of the scene.

For some years now we have stayed with the usage 'Manor Gardens Centre', with Manor Gardens Welfare Trust as the legal term for the Charity as it is registered. In this book I either use the term 'Manor Gardens Centre' or often just 'the Centre'. Along with our logo, we also use the strap line 'for health and community services'.

Personal names
The most important issue here is the naming of women. For much of the twentieth century married and unmarried women were referred to just as 'Mrs Jones' or 'Miss Smith', unmarried women were more likely to have their first names added. The use of husbands' initials or names was preferred by married women of the upper and middle classes, and some people continue to use this format. Thus we have Mrs W.B. Keen and Mrs Edgar Davis.

Personal names were generally used less than today. Florence Keen continued to write to her long-standing friend Domini Crosfield as 'My Dear Lady Crosfield' to the last. Only at home and among intimates would she be called by the familiar versions of her name: Flo and Flossie. In some cases I had to look hard to discover what first names were; some I never found out. In keeping with our times I have used the given names of our main protagonists, especially Florence Keen, Domini Crosfield and Althea Davis.

Discriminatory terms
We have become more sensitive and more egalitarian in our use of language and descriptive terms for groups of people and their conditions. Nowhere is this

sensitivity more acute than in the voluntary sector. Sometimes, at an experimental stage, these new usages can seem awkward and easy to make fun of, but we are often satisfied and grateful in the longer run. Instances are common in the field of mental health. Old terms are dropped when they are felt to be disparaging or are largely used in pejorative senses, such as 'lunatic', 'idiot', 'hysteric', even 'backward' and compare the relatively short life of 'spastic' for a physical condition. It is not easy to negotiate the complex classifications, scientific and popular, for conditions of age, size, mobility, skin colour and so on. Some terms people may use of themselves, but may not be comfortably used by others. We begin to feel awkward now with 'geriatric', and even 'disability', 'senile' and others. There will never be complete or lasting consensus.

The gendering of terms has been a major issue within the women's movement. The most obvious has been the challenge to the use of the word 'man', especially as a prefix or suffix, to assume gender inclusiveness ('mankind') or worse to imply gender exclusiveness ('craftsman'). Probably most organisations have taken a conscious decision on the use of 'Chairman' or 'Chair'. 'Chairman' is used so much and for so long that I have kept it unless there has been a conscious change or I am making my own generalisation. At the Centre Noreen Nicholson was the first member of the Board of Trustees to ask to be called 'Chair', in 2002.

Changes in Health Services in the twentieth century

One of the strands of this story is the gradual, and then in the case of the NHS, revolutionary, change in the provision of health services in this country throughout the twentieth century. It may be helpful to sketch this history here for the many of us who do not normally think about the world of health before the NHS. This is especially relevant to the currently increased level of public interest and concern with what is going to happen to the NHS, the theme of 'privatisation', return to reliance on 'market forces' and what alternatives there might be.

When the twentieth century began, and our story begins, the state or national level of provision for health and social care services was largely confined to public health, for example infrastructural investment that would release us from the epidemics of cholera and typhoid fever. Even here, municipal and private investment played an important part.

In the area of Islington in 1900 all hospitals were private entities, supported by philanthropic public contributions, raised constantly with great expense of effort. The wills of the rich frequently start with legacies to hospitals. Dispensaries, providing lower cost medicines, were either private, charitable or municipal. Institutions such as prisons and workhouses were local responsibilities. Schools received almost no attention in the field of health inspection or care. The Borough of Islington had a single Medical Officer of Health. These officials who had been in place for the last third of the nineteenth century were of the greatest importance for the development of improved policies and provision. Dr Harris the Islington MOH from 1891-1921 was an important ally in the setting up of the Centre in 1913.

INTRODUCTION

The policies of the Liberal Government (1906-15) and the radical new outlook following the First World War led to continuous changes and improvements in public health care provision. Again the local authorities were chiefly responsible for implementation. It was not until 1919 that a Ministry of Health was formed. By 1940 the nation's health services were an unsatisfactory patchwork and varied greatly in quality. Ideas that were to lead to the formation of the NHS were already being discussed in the late 1930s and were accelerated by the Second World War. They were negotiated and shaped by the Labour Government elected in 1945 with Aneurin Bevan as the Minister of Health. The NHS Act of 1946 came into force on 5 July 1948.

The Author

I need to enter a word of warning. The author is an academic social anthropologist, with a historical inclination, used to the discipline of critical and impartial writing. Good scholarship does not always require impersonality or anonymity however. But in this case the author is also fully engaged with his subject matter as an actor in the process. I have lived in Islington, north and south, since 1964, with a few years spent overseas. I was active in community politics in the early 1970s as part of what some called 'the tenants movement' at a time when the housing crisis had reached a critical point. In recent years I have been Chair of the Islington Children's Fund (2002-06). I joined the Board of the Manor Gardens Centre in 2004 and was elected Chair in 2006. It is in all our interests that we should assess our record accurately, critically and as dispassionately as possible. Nevertheless, this author is a committed enthusiast and partisan for the cause. In this spirit I hope the book will serve to express our respect and gratitude to all those who came before us and have left us such a wonderful heritage.

PART ONE

Foundation

Manor Gardens

Prior to the 1840s, the area of Manor Gardens was pastureland belonging to the moated manor house that was situated close to the site of the Odeon Cinema. It was first known as Manor Road. The name of the street is now Manor Gardens.

It is a short street leading off Holloway Road or the A1, for centuries the main access road from the North to the city of London and its markets. Manor Gardens is short but it has a disproportionate amount of historical interest. At first it was a residential road with a number of substantial but not grand early Victorian semi-detached villas and their modest gardens. The *Ordnance Survey* map of Upper Holloway of 1869 shows three semi-detached villas and one large house on the north side and two semi-detached villas and five detached houses with more substantial gardens, on the south side. Of these only the two semi-detached villas occupied by the Manor Gardens Centre survive.

Holloway Road, c.1905. The Marlborough Theatre (opened 1903, demolished 1962), is on the right. The theatre was replaced by an office block called Marlborough House, subsequently used by the University of North London.

The Great Northern Hospital, Holloway Road, in 1886.

In the late nineteenth-century two important buildings were constructed on the corners of Manor Gardens with Holloway Road. The Great Northern Hospital was opened in April 1888, completed in 1894. In 1921 the Hospital was granted the title Royal Northern Hospital. The St David's Wing, opened in 1931 and completed in 1935, was built on the north side of Manor Gardens running from near Holloway Road to the edge of the present Manor Gardens Centre estate.

The Holloway Empire Theatre opened in 1899. Until 1915 it was a Music Hall where Marie Lloyd who lived nearby, performed, along with George Robey and others. It became a cinema in 1915. It has been rebuilt twice since.

On 20 September 1906 the Islington North Library, largely financed by a gift from the American philanthropist Andrew Carnegie, was opened on the south side. It was the first public library in Islington. In 1911 the extraordinarily large building now known as the Beaux-Arts Building from its architectural style, was built by the GPO as its Money Order headquarters.

North Islington in 1913

What motivated the founders of the North Islington Infant Welfare Centre and School for Mothers to start their work in 1913? What were the health and welfare needs of the poorer people in North Islington in the early twentieth-century? How were they being met? Let us set the scene.

The boundaries of North Islington were much as they are now, but the area south of the Angel was the separate borough of Finsbury which was incorporated into the Borough of Islington in 1965. North Islington is just south of the affluent village of Highgate on either side of the A1 or Great North Road. Its population was very dense, and in 1911 at its highest 412,994, more than twice the size of the current Islington and Finsbury boroughs combined now. This was a size similar to Belfast, Edinburgh or Newcastle at the time. Even today at about 200,000, the population of Islington is considerably larger than many large towns in the South of England such as Swindon or Bournemouth. By 1900 the whole borough had been built up, with very few dedicated open spaces left. Most people lived in privately rented accommodation. There was very little municipal or philanthropic housing in Upper Holloway.

'Upper Holloway' is a loose term that refers chiefly to the area between Archway to the north and Seven Sisters Road and Parkhurst Road to the south, and stretching at its widest to the neighbouring Boroughs of Camden in the west and Haringey and Hackney in the east. Lower Holloway continues to Highbury Corner. Upper Holloway was built on the lower slopes of Highgate Hill and its relatively elevated position was described in the first part of the nineteenth century as being most 'salubrious' and having 'a bracing atmosphere'. By 1913 it was far from a salubrious or generally healthy place. Jones Brothers store (now Waitrose and still part of the John Lewis Partnership) began in a small way in 1867, building up the well-to-do 'carriage trade' from all parts of London. By 1892 it had 500 employees, but the general social decline of Holloway prevented them extending their fine building.

Then as now Islington was characterised by a mixture of poor and better off households in each ward. Today Upper Holloway offers a rather misleading visual guide to its social history. Just about every trace of its poorest housing has gone. Most have been replaced by islands of council housing, often in blocks of flats. Other poorer areas have become open spaces such as Whittington Park. The surviving nineteenth-century streets, mainly of three-storey terraced housing need some interpretation. They were designed for clerks and artisans, respectable and fully employed working and lower middle-class families. The typical house and way of life of one of these, the fictitious Mr Charles Pooter, rather at the socially grander end of that scale, is described in *The Diary of a Nobody* (1892) by George and Weedon Grossmith. But much of this kind of housing soon became, or even started off as multi-occupied dwellings with minimal amenities: an outside privy, a tin tub brought in for a bath in front of the fire, and maybe a wash bowl and some cooking facility on the landings. What often happened was that houses built speculatively in the 1850s and 1860s were not completed for twenty years or so. Meanwhile the streets were unpaved, unlit and full of uncollected rubbish. Such conditions were at their worst in the 1930s when there was an average of eleven people to a six-room house. Campbell Road, off Seven Sisters Road not far from the Holloway Road, was notorious as 'Campbell Bunk' 'the worst street in North London' (see

White 1986). A large building in the street, intended to be a Public House, became a 'common lodging house' for 90 men - a very profitable form of renting for the landlord. Such conditions were common up to the 1970s when large parts of Upper Holloway were declared 'housing action zones'.

Manor Gardens Centre has always kept good statistics of its activities. For several years we have a record of the occupations of the fathers of children brought to the Centre They give a good profile of the range of jobs they had. For some time Upper Holloway had been known for its small workshops, artisans and craftsmen in a great variety of trades. There were a few small factories. The growth of railways and trams, the Post Office and other services provided many of the better, more secure jobs. At the lower end of the scale of wealth and employment was the sweated labour of women in such work as the laundries. The Anti-Sweating League reported in August 1913 that half of the sweated labour comprised married women. 'The infant mortality in the district known as "laundry-land" (in northern Islington) was excessively heavy'. This was attributed to the absence for 14-15 hours a day of the mothers. The LCC paid 'charladies' 5 pence per hour in 1913; the laundry rate was a maximum of 3 pence. Many men were employed only on a casual basis and not a few lived by fringe activities some of them criminal. A school leaver might earn 5-8 shillings per week, two pence or less an hour.

The Sutton Dwellings (1924) opposite the Town Hall had an upper limit of 25 shillings per week for a family to qualify for application. Rents for this relatively 'luxurious' accommodation for a poor working-class family were from two to eight shillings per week inclusive of rates, taxes and chimney sweeping. This income limit is consistent with the findings of a Fabian Society study of women in Lambeth which was published in a pamphlet in 1913 (republished in 1980) by Maud Pember Reeves entitled *Round about a pound a week* [18-24 shillings]. This was based on actual expenditure of working-class families with stable marriages and husband employed full time. In 1917 the average income of all families attending the Centre was £1.12 shillings. In the early days of the clinic, training exercises were held on household budgeting, starting at a pound a week, and later also at up to three pounds a week. In 1938/39 incomes after tax of up to about £3 per week accounted for 69% of all households in the country with another 28% in the £150-500 range (i.e. from three to about ten pounds a week) the combined total being 97%. Only 1% of the population had incomes above £1,000 per annum (Beveridge). Given the lack of open space and increasing regulation, opportunities for supplementing incomes from allotments or domestic piggeries and henhouses were rare. As the history of Campbell Road shows there were good opportunities for scavenging, recycling, petty trading and also petty theft, some of which were combined.

The clientele of the Manor Gardens Centre mostly fell into William Booth's wealth categories on a scale from A ('occasional labourer, loafers, semi-criminal') to F ('high class labourer'). Such definitions are always changing but the terms 'poor' and 'working-class' characterise the great majority of the people for whom the Manor Gardens Centre has provided services. In 1900 Seebohm Rowntree had reported that the proportion of 'poor' in London was approximately 30% who together with over 50% 'comfortable working-class' made up over 82% of the population of London.

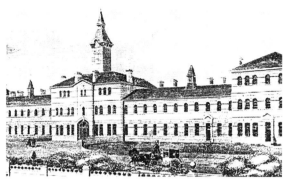

St Mary Islington Workhouse in St John's Road.

The Victorian Poor Laws, regularly amended, were not suspended until 1929 for the most part, and finally in 1945. In 1913 there were 8,629 'paupers' living in workhouses in Islington, some 2.6% of the population. There were two workhouses in the immediate area of Manor Gardens Centre: the City Workhouse at the northern end of Cornwallis Road, which had 611 local paupers, and the (Islington) St Mary's Parish Workhouse. People would do anything they could to stay out of the workhouse. There were at least as many desperately poor outside, for example those who used the regular soup kitchens and received the 8,500 Christmas dinners, distributed by the Mayor of Islington in 1912 'for the poor of the Borough of Islington'.

Who was doing anything to alleviate the effect of poverty on the health of mothers and their babies, very young children and their families? Of course at the most intimate level many mothers and fathers did all they could. The combined efforts of the Great Northern Hospital, the Salvation Army, the workhouse and a few others gave some help variously to single mothers, mothers in childbirth or with sick children. But what the parents lacked so often was the best knowledge of how to look after and raise their babies in a healthy way in terms of diet, clothing, exercise, fresh air and sunlight and hygiene.

Political contexts

Public debate about the health of mothers and babies, infant mortality and the long decline in the birth rate received new impetus in the early twentieth-century. The British army had performed badly in the so-called 'Boer War' in South Africa that came to an end in 1902. There was great concern about the health of young British men. Of those volunteering to fight 40% were deemed unfit; many of those accepted were below par. Unfavourable comparison was made with Germany, a major imperial rival. This issue attracted the attention of Conservative politicians and connected with other currents of concern from far left to far right. In 1902 an Act was passed requiring training of midwives. A Report on Physical Deterioration was published in 1904. In 1906 there was a National Conference on Infant Mortality that led to the formation of the National Association for the Prevention of Infant Mortality and the promotion of the welfare of children under school age. But it was the social policies of the Liberal governments of Campbell-Bannerman and Asquith from 1906-15 that began a round of essential reforms.

FOUNDATION

Among the achievements of the Liberal government were various pieces of legislation concerning pensions and insurance, notably Asquith's [Health] Insurance Act of 1911, which removed fear of the workhouse from many poor working-class families. The so-called 'People's Budget' of 1909 introduced a 'super tax' on incomes over £5,000, equivalent to about £250,000 in today's terms. The standard rate of tax was one shilling and two pence in the pound or about 5.8%. This was something of a watershed in taxation history, but while the very poor did not pay income tax, the working man, in 1912, paid more in indirect taxation than he might receive in benefits, through taxes on beer and cigarettes especially.

By 1891 primary education from the age of five had become available, compulsory and free. In 1906 free school meals became available. In 1907 The Notification of Birth Act (made compulsory in 1915) encouraged notification of all births (live or dead) which allowed authorities to contact mothers at an early stage. In the same year, the Liberal government introduced a school medical service (especially inspection for head lice) and free meals for the needy. Fine school buildings close to the Centre such as Duncombe, Grafton, Montem and Yerbury still survive; many others have now closed or been converted into dwellings. In 1913 all were in full use with class sizes at least double their present numbers. A sign of the poverty of many was that one school held a benefit concert to raise money to provide 'boots for poor children' who might otherwise go to school without shoes. A public appeal in 1917 by the Ragged Schools Union and the Shaftesbury Society for the London Poor Children's Boot Society resulted in 15,205 pairs of boots being distributed in Islington alone. The boots had to be specially marked to prevent them being sold or pawned.

Health and welfare services available to mothers and their babies were a ragged patchwork that covered a small proportion. The (Islington) St Mary's Parish Workhouse in Upper Holloway had an infirmary and a dispensary. The Salvation Army had a hostel for a few single women and their children. There was an Islington Charities Association whose committee organised occasional benefit events, and provided Christmas dinners and soup kitchens in Upper Holloway. Public Baths such as the fine new Hornsey Road Baths made a good contribution to preventative health and hygiene. These were the largest in the borough and had separate first and second-class baths for men and women, 145 slipper baths and washhouse accommodation for 49.

The Great Northern Hospital on Holloway Road opened a ward in 1909 with 12 cots for children under five. It offered some free services and gave emergency care, but even its discounted charges were outside the capability of most Manor Gardens Centre clients. It struggled to keep going itself although it was probably the largest charity in Islington. It held a formal fund raising dinner in 1913 and raised a staggering total of £4,342. This was front-page news in the *Islington Gazette*.

Much of this charitable giving resulted in handouts of temporary and limited value. More importantly, none of these worthy efforts could offer what the Centre was to provide:

FOUNDATION

a) A specific focus on babies and young children up to school age (five) and their mothers. Apart from the immediate period of childbirth, and not always then, these categories of need were ignored by the state or borough health systems.

b) Concern for the education and training of mothers and parents.

c) Preventative measures, such as hygiene, light, ventilation and diet.

The Centre first started in 1913, on a rent-free basis, at the Highgate Presbyterian Church Mission hall, now the Africa Centre, in Elthorne Road near Archway. It later returned to open a branch there. When it had to make room for refugees from Belgium after the first few months of the war, it moved for a few months to the nearby Baptist Church on Holloway Road. The Bishop of Islington was a leading signatory to the Centre's public appeal in 1914. During the 1920s the wife of the Bishop of Islington was active on our committee. And in 1965 we were honoured and stimulated by a visit by Archbishop Trevor Huddleston. But on the whole religious organisations do not feature largely in the Manor Gardens Centre story.

The most catastrophic feature of the health of young children in Britain in 1913 was the high rate of infant mortality, that is the number of babies born alive who died before the age of one. The Centre's Public Appeal of 30 November 1914 showed the following comparative figures:

Chidren dying before their first birthday 1905-10

Hampstead	72 per 1,000
Islington	110 "
Shoreditch	151 "

The extremes are broadly similar to those across the country, for example in 1914:

Oxfordshire	73 per 1,000
Glamorgan	154 "

In 1916 the Centre began reporting comparative figures for Islington:

Children dying before their first birthday 1916

	all children	children attending Manor Gardens Centre
Tufnell Park	103 per 1,000	24 per thousand
Upper Holloway	107 "	58 "
Tollington	136 "	37 "

Diseases mostly likely to cause the death of infants included bronchitis, pneumonia, diarrhoeal diseases and convulsions. Other serious diseases and conditions included rickets, whooping cough (pertussis), tuberculosis, measles, scarlet fever, diphtheria and chicken pox. We shall return to these. Underlying causes were malnutrition and poor hygiene. Some major epidemic diseases had been successfully brought under control, such as smallpox (through vaccination) and cholera (through public health measures).

The early twentieth century was a lively time in the history of what we now call 'gender politics', of which an important instance was the Women's Suffrage Movement. An outstanding characteristic of the history of Manor Gardens Welfare Centre, which we shall treat further below, is that for many decades it was staffed and managed almost entirely by women professionals and volunteers. It might be argued that there is a natural affinity between these women and the subject of their work, but this is insufficient to account for or understand their motivation and success. Most of them were married, though not all had children. Some had political connections, mostly of a Liberal or Radical-Liberal tendency. The Centre itself did not involve itself directly in the political movement though no doubt many of the staff were sympathetic to the cause of women's rights to vote and related forms of equality. It is a sad irony that in 1913 within half a mile of Manor Gardens and the Holloway soup kitchens, Emmeline Pankhurst and three other suffragettes were on hunger strike in Holloway Prison and being forcibly fed after their protests. In that year under an Act of 1884 only men were enfranchised and only 37% of them. First partly enfranchised in 1919, by 1929 women formed rather more than half of an electorate that had quadrupled.

In 1916 the Centre received a gift from the 'Highgate Branch of the London Women's Suffragette Movement'.

Setting up the Centre
Florence Keen and friends

By 1913 'Schools for Mothers' or 'Mothers and Infants Welfare Centres' had become a small social movement in England. An Association of Infant Consultation and Schools for Mothers was set up in 1911. This was part of the National League for Physical Education and Improvement which in 1930 became the Association of Infant Welfare and Maternity Centres. There were about 100 such Centres in the UK in 1913 of which a quarter or more were under municipal control. In London they were in Finsbury - whose MOH Dr George Newman had published a report in 1906 entitled *Infant mortality: a social problem* - in St Pancras close by, in Deptford, Lambeth and Woolwich and a few other places. All those in London were completely voluntary.

The first such centre in England was established in June 1907 as the St Pancras Mothers and Infants Society at 6-7 Chalton Street in Somers Town, just off Euston Road on the site of what is now a Novotel. The Hon. Secretaries were Miss Evelyn Buntin and Dr John Sykes, Medical Officer of Health for the Borough of St Pancras (now part of the Borough of Camden). The Hon. Medical Officer was Dr Dora Buntin. Dr Sykes was already promoting ideas for such initiatives, but the specific inspiration came from Alys Russell, estranged first wife of the philosopher Bertrand Russell.

She was an American Quaker. She had visited Ghent in Belgium with a party of women members of a Co-operative Socialist group. The infant mortality rate in Ghent was 350 per thousand, more than twice that of the worst part of London. Alys was impressed by the work of the Belgian socialists in setting up Mother and Child centres and adapted it in St Pancras.

Alys Russell was a friend of Nora Hobhouse, whose husband was Leonard Hobhouse the first Professor of Sociology at the London School of Economics. Mrs Hobhouse was a neighbour and friend in Highgate of Florence Keen. She was involved in the setting up of the Centre in Manor Gardens in its planning stages and was a joint Hon. Secretary with Florence Keen. After her death in 1925 her husband donated a sunlight lamp in her memory and she is referred to in the Annual Report as 'one of our founders'. After Florence Keen's death in 1942 however, it is Florence who is referred to as 'Founder', in the singular.

In any case Florence Keen was the prime mover in setting up the North Islington Centre. She had lived in Highgate in the fine house *Mayfield* at No. 35 West Hill since about 1890. Her second son was born there in 1891. In 1913 her older sons were aged 24 and 22, her twin daughters 17 and her youngest son 11. By then her parents and those of her husband had died. It has not been ascertained what they might have inherited, but in any case her husband William Brock Keen (1859-1941), an accountant, was already a very wealthy man on his own account. Florence was well established in the highest echelons of Highgate society. She had time on her hands so to say. She was strong, energetic, intelligent and wealthy. She combined charm and loyalty with a certain fierceness of manner. She was said to have had a great sense of fun but little sense of humour. Her mother's father, Sir John Heaton, a Leeds man, had been Chief Medical Officer for the London County Council. She is said to have voted Liberal and her husband Conservative. As to religious affiliation, her family has said that she was agnostic. The Keen family seem to have been Baptists and Florence's parental families were also non-conformist. Both Florence and William clearly had some notion of commitment to public service, but we know nothing about any previous philanthropic activity. Her personal circle or network of friends and acquaintances was quite extraordinary. Wealth and residence in Highgate allowed access to numerous 'titled' people, nobility, aristocracy and even indirectly to royalty.

Florence Keen had been discussing and developing the idea of setting up a 'School for Mothers' some time before the decision was finally made in late 1913. She had been talking to Islington's longstanding Medical Officer of Health, Dr Alfred Edwin Harris. He was in post in Islington from 1891-1921 and had advocated such measures for some time without success. For example he tried unsuccessfully in 1906 to persuade the council to employ Health Visitors. She would have spoken with doctors from the Great Northern Hospital and the Islington Board of Guardians, and of course with her friends in Highgate and beyond. The first record of a meeting is in the *Islington Gazette* reporting a gathering in Mrs Keen's house on Friday 17 October 1913.This was a watershed meeting in terms of mobilising a wider group of potential supporters and making a public appeal for financial support. It is clear however that the details had already been agreed and the key workers had volunteered.

The newspaper report refers to 'a drawing room meeting' at Mrs Keen's home *Mayfield* which was attended by 'over 150 ladies and gentlemen interested in the movement'. Twenty names are given. The chair was taken by Frances Lady Chelmsford whose husband Lord Chelmsford GCMS (1868-1933) was later to be Viceroy of India. She had just returned from Australia where her husband had been Governor of New South Wales. She had seen excellent infant care there and on her return she had accepted an invitation to be President of the St Pancras School for Mothers. She was glad to help another School in Islington 'where it was so urgently needed'. Lady Chelmsford knew Lady Islington, wife of John Dickson Poynder, 1st Baron of Islington who had been Governor of New Zealand while she had been in New South Wales. Lady Islington was to be an active supporter of the Centre. She would have come to know of the Plunket Society and the work of Dr Truby King, of whom more later.

There were a few other titled ladies including Hermione, Countess Ferrers (1891-1969) wife of the 12th Earl of Ferrers. She was only 22 years old at the time. Another distinguished couple were Mr and Mrs David Sydney Waterlow MP (later Sir David and Lady Waterlow). He was the son of Sir Sydney Waterlow who endowed the community in 1889 with his fine 26 acre park on the southern slope of Highgate Hill, calling it 'a garden for the gardenless'. It is now known as Waterlow Park. Mrs Waterlow had already been an active fund-raiser for the Great Northern Hospital. She urged the need for infant care and stressed the importance of prevention rather than cure.

A Doctor Waller who was present struck a progressive and rather amusing note that was rewarded with approving calls of 'Hear, Hear!' 'He said that a tremendous lot of cant was talked about the undesirables among the poorer classes, and the waste of helping them. As a matter of fact there were more undesirables among the so-called upper classes. What was really wanted, he remarked, was a school for people of both sexes.'

There were several medical or medically related people present including Dr A.E. Harris the MOH, Dr Morrison physician to the Great Northern Hospital, Miss Michael a member of the Islington Board of Guardians, and two 'lady sanitary inspectors'. Of the others, two stand out who were to be stalwart supporters, officers and committee members of the Centre for many years: Mrs Ada (Audrey) Wallas and Mrs Nora Hobhouse, wives of two famous radical intellectuals and academics, Graham Wallas and Leonard Hobhouse, and both of them personal friends of Florence Keen.

The young Hermione Countess Ferrers made a clever appeal for funds. With a wider audience in mind she declared that 'no-one need hesitate in contributing half-a-crown if they were unable to give a guinea'. [In today's terms something like £5 and £50.] 'There was no other investment that would give them a handsomer

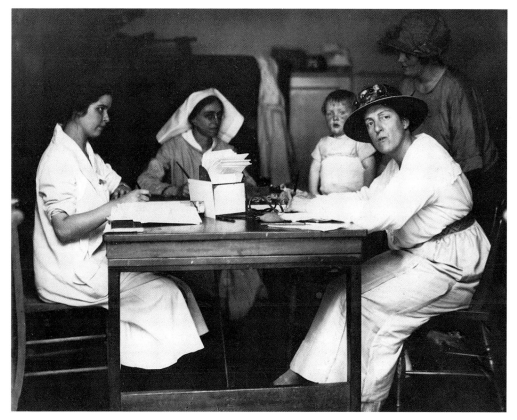

Dr Vance Knox, on the right, in 1914.

return for their money'. Lady Wolmar had offered £10 if four others would give the same (applause). Mr David Waterlow proposed a vote of thanks to Lady Chelmsford and Mr and Mrs Keen.

The Presbyterian Church in Highgate offered space in their Mission Hall in Elthorne Road off Holloway Road near Archway. In November 1913 the work of the Centre began. Dr Vance Knox, a female doctor from Highgate offered to give one day per week to run a free clinic. In the first week nine mothers attended. Mrs Keen reportedly stood in the street wearing a sandwich board and touting for custom.

A year later on 30 November 1914 the North Islington School for Mothers submitted a petition to the Council of the Borough of Islington. It was a three-page document signed by the Bishop of Islington and 96 'influential ratepayers'. The final sentence read:

'The advance of medical science has brought home to all educated people the importance of the first year of human life, and has shown that on the treatment of the baby during that time the future health of the man or women will, in many cases, depend.'

Work grew fast and soon 70-80 mothers attended each Friday. Good results were soon to be seen. The Board of Education made a small grant, but in that first

The Dispensary at Manor Gardens in 1920.

year the total cash expenditure was only £110. The second year budget was £472. This would support a six-day a week service in permanent premises. More than half the sum was for nurses' salaries. Additional funds were requested from the Borough Council and the Health Authority. In 1914 Exchequer grants were made available to selected voluntary agencies which could receive up to 50% of their approved annual expenditure.

By this time the committee of the 'North Islington School for Mothers' had 19 members of whom 8 we know were among those attending the meeting in October 1913. Dr Alice Vance Knox and Dr Jessie Campbell were the Honorary Medical Officers and were to remain so for many years. Nurse Smith was the all-important 'Lady Superintendent'. Mrs Keen was Honorary Treasurer and Acting Secretary together with Nora Hobhouse.

Domini Crosfield

Lady Domini Crosfield (1890-1963) might just possibly have been party to discussions about setting up the Centre. She is first recorded as a 'subscriber' in 1916 and in 1919, aged 27, she became President. She held this position for forty years until 1959 and remained actively interested in the Centre until her death in 1963. She was a widow for the last twenty-five years of this exceptional fifty years or so of involvement with the Centre. She was born in 1892 into the well-to-do

FOUNDATION

Anglo-Hellenic Elliadi family. She married Arthur Crosfield (1865-1938) at the age of seventeen in 1909. It was his second marriage.

Arthur Crosfield had inherited the thriving soap manufacturing company of Joseph Crosfield and Sons Ltd. at the Bank Quay Works in Warrington on the river Mersey in Lancashire. This had been set up by his grandfather Joseph Crosfield, a Quaker, in 1814. Arthur built up the firm, acquiring the UK rights to the American brand Persil in 1909. In 1911 he sold the company which in 1919 became a subsidiary of Lever Brothers, later Leverhulme, which kept the Crosfield company name until it was sold in turn to ICI in 1997. Arthur had bought a fine house then called *Parkfield* at 43 West Hill, Highgate in 1910. This was just up the hill on the same side as No. 35 *Mayfield*, the home of Florence Keen. Following the sale of his firm he was able to spend a million pounds on restoring and expanding the house which he named *Witanhurst* (a rendering back into Saxon of 'parliament hill'). By 1913 the house was ready for its purpose as one of the grandest and most hospitable private houses in London.

A further significance of the sale of Joseph Crosfield and Sons to the Lever Bros. conglomerate was that the Crosfield family were friendly with Lord Leverhulme and his second wife the Viscountess Leverhulme. Lord Leverhulme died in 1925 but his wife continued to attend fundraising receptions at Witanhurst in the 1920s and after. Lord Leverhulme's estate continued to make an annual donation until the 1990s.

Arthur Crosfield was elected as Liberal MP for Warrington, where he was known as a good employer, in the Liberal landslide 1906 election. He was defeated in 1910 but remained active in Liberal circles. He was awarded a baronetcy in 1915. This gave an important fillip to the standing of the Crosfields; from now on it was as 'Lady Crosfield' that Domini was most widely known.

Domini Crosfield stood unsuccessfully as Liberal candidate in General Elections for North Islington in 1929 and 1931 and for Finchley in 1930.

In the twenty years between the wars Domini Crosfield devoted her considerable talent and energy to develop the social life of *Witanhurst*, especially in the form of tennis and garden parties, and concerts. *Witanhurst* in the 1920s-30s has been described as 'a magnet for royalty, statesmen, intellectuals, musicians and sporting greats'. Every year the Crosfields held tennis tournaments and exhibition matches at their home. Their chief purpose was philanthropic fundraising. They gave generously to many causes including the British Legion (of which Sir Arthur's brother Lt. Colonel George Crosfield was a co-founder), the Royal Northern Hospital, Save the Children, the National Playing Fields Association (of which Sir Arthur was the first Chairman) and the Boy Scouts (a favourite charity of Princess Alice of Athlone, a good friend of Lady Crosfield). But over the years the chief beneficiary was the Manor Gardens Centre.

The house at *Witanhurst* played an important role in the history of the Centre. The oldest part dates to about 1700. It stood in 14 acres of ground when Crosfield bought it from Walter Scrimgeour, a stockbroker. It is part of the prehistoric

The Crosfield soap factory in Warrington in 1886.

landscape of the eastern slopes of Hampstead Heath. It has a view of *Kenwood House*. It now has 5.5 acres of garden and the house is currently described as a Grade II listed 'pastiche Queen Anne' palace. It had more than 90 rooms with over 30 bedrooms, 8 living rooms, a 70-foot ballroom, a music room with three grand pianos and four tennis courts (two hard, two grass). The house became very expensive to maintain. One economy was the use of light bulbs of a maximum 20 watts. Parts of it were used by the Royal Air Force during the second World War. In later years it was poorly maintained. Domini let out some flats to friends including Mme Venizelou, the violinist Yehudi Menuhin and his family, and the wife of the Czech Ambassador. Nonetheless Domini Crosfield resumed fundraising parties after the war up to 1960, three years before her death in 1963. Her personal estate at death was valued at £129,937. Her adopted son Paul George Homer Crosfield - an adopted son of a Greek cousin who came to England as a refugee - sold the property in 1970 for £1,200,000. In the 1980s potential buyers were rumoured to include King Hussein of Jordan and Vice-President Assad of Syria. At the time of writing the house has been purchased by an unnamed buyer, probably Russian, for a reported £50,000,000 and is being massively refurbished.

Arthur Crosfield was the genial and generous host, tending to remain rather in the background. He was a liberal and non-conformist with an interest in both national and local charitable work. Like his wife he was a keen sportsman and musician. He won the French Amateur Golf Championship and was Chairman of the National Playing Fields Association. He played a leading role in the successful campaign to keep *Kenwood House* and its 130-acre estate in the public domain. He was Chairman of the Kenwood Committee in 1919. It was opened to the public in 1925 by King George V. He was briefly a governor of Highgate Boys' School. He had a special interest in the Balkans, shared by his wife. He published a book in 1922 on *The Settlement of the Near East* and maintained an extensive correspondence with Lloyd-George on the subject.

Domini's adult life was at first totally circumscribed by her husband's wealth and social ambition, and the demands of being the chatelaine of *Witanhurst*. As it happened they were not to have children. This enabled her to devote her energy and affection to her philanthropic work, and especially to the aims of the Centre. She was a tall, lean and strong woman with a confident social presence and considerable charm. She was an exceptionally good tennis player. At the age of 19 she reached the finals of the tennis championship in St Moritz in the singles (three sets), the doubles and mixed doubles. In the same year, 1911, she was semi-finalist on clay at Monte Carlo. The next six years were not propitious for international tennis but it picked up soon after the war. Tennis was by and large a sport for the well-to-do in those days, favoured as a social game by the aristocracy and royalty. Wimbledon built its new stands in 1922. In 1927 Domini, now aged 35, won the singles and double finals of the international championships held in Switzerland. Her annual fundraising tennis parties will be discussed later on.

Domini's other great passion was music. She was an accomplished pianist, and played in some of the concerts she organised at Witanhurst. She also joined in Christmas parties in Manor Gardens, playing the upright piano while Florence recited and William Keen sang. She was friendly with many musicians and dancers and supported musical causes. She was Vice-President and a Director of the London Philharmonic Society. Two of her most distinguished musical friends were Yehudi Menuhin and Margot Fonteyn. As an athlete and sportswoman, as well as having a strong interest in dance, she keenly encouraged the Centre's work in the field of movement and physical exercise. She wrote a small book on *The Dances of Greece* in 1948 which was written in association with the National Association for Physical Education in the UK.

Domini Crosfield (née Elliadi) maintained a life-long interest in Greece. She was born a British citizen but was conscious of her Greek ancestry. She was given a Greek Orthodox funeral. She was to receive the Order of the Phoenix from the Greek state. Others of the few recipients of this level of distinction include Stavros Niarchos and Patrick Leigh-Fermor. One of her great friends was a Greek woman Helena Venizelou (née Skylitsi 1875-1959). She was the second wife of Eleftherios Venizelos (1864-1936). They were married at *Witanhurst*. He was a republican and revolutionary who opposed the Greek monarchy and became Prime Minister 1910-15, 1917-20, 1924, and 1928-33. She was a generous supporter of the Centre and bequeathed £1,000 at her death in 1959.

It is an intriguing irony that this close friend should have been the wife of a revolutionary anti-monarchist when so many other of her friends were of royal families from several European nations and, as we shall see, especially the House of Windsor. One of the rich neighbours of Domini and Florence Keen was an American Mrs Nancy Leeds. She inherited the great sum of $400 million from her husband, a tin magnate, which made her one of the richest women in London, and probably the richest widow. She lived in rented accommodation in *Kenwood House* in Highgate. Mrs Leeds understandably had a wide social circle. This included for some years, discreetly, Prince Christian of Denmark youngest son of George I King of the Hellenes and uncle to the present Duke of Edinburgh. Following the assassination of Prince Christian's father, his elder brother ruled as King from 1913-17 and 1920-23. On her marriage to Prince Christian on 1 January 1920 Mrs Nancy Leeds became HRH Princess Anastasia of Greece and Denmark. She died of cancer in August 1923. Before her marriage Nancy Leeds had become a generous patron of the Centre. A conservatory building where the children could play in wet weather was named after her. This was for a long time known as The Leeds Shelter. She was also instrumental in involving the American Women's Club of London, whose long-term co-operation with the Centre will be discussed later. It was also no doubt in part due to her that the American Red Cross made a significant grant to the Centre.

PART TWO

Success Story

Managing the Centre
The Centre's values and vision

The leadership and management worked hard for the growth and excellence of the Centre. It steadily increased its financial support, the number of its volunteer workers and the range and quality of its services. It was conscious of itself as an innovator in the field of child health and the education of mothers in childcare; fathers too were involved. It publicly stated its intention to become a 'model centre'. It has always been willing to share its values and experience and co-operate with the similar if smaller centres that grew up in Islington within five years of its founding. It co-operated with the Islington Borough Council from the start and has never ceased to do so. The Centre has always been concerned to maintain contact with its supporters, especially by means of a comprehensive Annual Report. In the early days this was charged to non-subscribers at sixpence in 1916, rising to one shilling in 1918 and two shillings by 1920.

The Centre's partners in the early days also included the British Medical Association, the King's Fund, the London Federation of Infant Welfare Centres and the North London Midwives Association. From 1919 the Centre was periodically inspected by the Ministry of Health. On 12 July 1921 the Centre received a letter expressing:

'appreciation of the valuable work done for the benefit of the mothers and children attending the Centre.

[The Minister] is glad to note that the development of the Centre has been carried out on sound lines and in accordance with the general recommendations of the Minister. He particularly observed the excellent organisation and equipment of the observation wards and the good results which have been obtained, and hopes that it will be possible to continue this branch of the work of the Centre, in spite of the inevitable high cost of maintenance'.

Again on 31 July 1929 the Centre received a letter from the Minister of Health expressing: 'appreciation of the high standard of work which is maintained at the Centre and of the ability and devotion which are displayed in its organisation'.

Florence Keen wrote in the second annual report that 'our Centre is part of a national movement the importance of which is recognised by the Government'. She sometimes expressed herself in poetic and philosophical terms. She spoke of richer and poorer being 'members of one another', a truth brought home especially during wartime. She reproduced a favourite motto at the head of the annual report taken from William Blake's poem Jerusalem:

Labour well the minute particulars, attend to the little ones,
And those who are in misery will not remain so long.

The Centre has been persistently optimistic and confident in the value and future potential of its work. The wartime periods were severely challenging, but the Centre adapted and survived. In 1923 the increase in unemployment and poverty among the local families was noted, and again in 1933 which was 'a heavy and difficult year'. 1937 was similarly reported as being 'a strenuous and difficult year'. However in the following year 'We can report progress, harmony and unanimity of purpose in every department'. The report on our 25th Anniversary in 1938 was a modest celebration, the 25 years of existence had not been 'devoid of anxieties and struggles, but nonetheless one of continuous progress and expansion in every phase of the work'.

As far as can be ascertained the Centre has always had an inclusive policy. This is more explicit and noticeable at present when gender, age, and ethnic background of staff and clientele are monitored and publicly recorded. There is a disturbing reference to nearby Stepney in 1929 when there were nine mothers and infants centres of which four were set up by Jewish people. The Stepney School

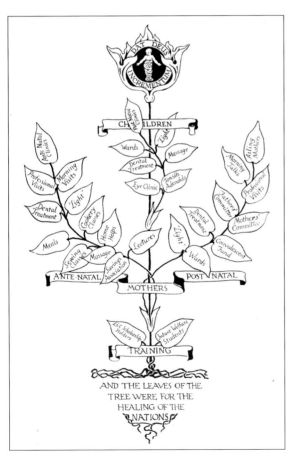

This 'tree diagram' was used in the 1920s and 1930s as a teaching aid and in the Annual Report. It encapsulates most of the methods, aims and aspirations of the period. Artist unknown. The rondel at the top is an altered representation of the Tondo on page 6 and has a Christian Latin motto. This was used on the cover of the Annual Report from 1922-1979.

for Mothers is said to have refused treatment to Jewish mothers. If so, this is discreditable, even if the rationale was that Jewish Centres already offered provision, or for that matter even if the Jewish Centres themselves were exclusionary. This would require further research to resolve. But it does raise questions, which are worth a separate discussion.

Racism and Eugenics

We have already introduced the theme of public and government concern for the health of the nation, especially of young men, in the context of a discourse on national superiority and empire building.

Early industrial capitalism had been exploitative and careless of human life in the extreme. People who had worked in factories from the age of seven or so were often unemployable by their mid-twenties. The workforce seemed endlessly replaceable. The notion of a 'wage slave' was a reality. Over the course of the nineteenth century a combination of self-interest, based changing needs for a fitter and more literate workforce and on moral pressures from politicians, Trade Unions and civil society, led to shorter working hours, higher wages and better conditions. Better, but still far from adequate.

When the issues of a healthier workforce and a healthier army converged, a new version of national interest emerged. When this was set in the context of imperial rivalry and conflict, the stakes were higher still.

A significant stream of thought that influenced the 'Infant Welfare' and 'Schools for Mothers' movement was that of eugenics. This was the name given by Professor Galton in London in the 1880s for a new science, based on the study of statistics rather than genetics, which had as its purpose the improvement of the 'racial stock' through selective encouragement and suppression of certain human traits. Misinterpretations of Darwin together with other vested ideologies soon combined his ideas with the social evolutionary and racist ideas that were current.

Galton's work became a kind of orthodoxy. In 1913 Karl Pearson, Professor of Eugenics at University College London, gave a public lecture in which he asserted that 'health and habits' of children and parents were fifteen times more significant than any other causes of infant mortality. Breeding and rearing were the issue. The fault lay largely with ignorant and irresponsible mothers, especially among the working-classes.

In the context of the history of the Manor Gardens Centre there is an interesting set of arguments about the nature of the rise of 'Schools for Mothers'. Was it a progressive movement led by enlightened and egalitarian women or was it in effect a kind of patriarchal and imperialist form of social control? The two documents are an article by the socialist feminist historian Anna Davin (1978) and an MA thesis by Linda Massie (1994) who worked at Manor Gardens Centre from 1984-92, becoming manager of the Women's Therapy Centre, and now a senior figure in the Department of Health working on the mental health and wellbeing of children. Of particular interest is that Anna Davin bases much of her argument on a reading of the record of the St Pancras School for Mothers, while Linda Massie takes the Manor Gardens Centre (in its first ten years as the North Islington School for Mothers) as her case study.

Davin documents the rhetoric of early twentieth-century participants in the 'health of the nation' debates. There was fear of 'national degeneration' and 'racial suicide'. Home was 'the cradle of the race', empire's first line of defence. The major newspapers, including *The Times*, adopted the imperial cause with enthusiasm. Closer to home, with less reserve, the *Islington Daily Gazette* issued a shocking editorial:

'The best bone, blood and sinew of this country is leaving our shores and being replaced by the stunted and weak-kneed alien. The seed of physical deterioration has been sown in this country, and it is developing at a pace which should concern with all seriousness every true patriot'.

Davin interprets the rise of Schools for Mothers as a strong instance of 'imperialism' and patriarchal domination and control of women in the interests of a national and racist agenda. Galton's almost religious belief in eugenics was part of the problem, despite the fact that some of the progressive parts of the women's movement (Suffragettes and Fabians) also had an interest in eugenics.

Linda Massie uses the more detailed archives of Manor Gardens Centre that Davin would not have known about, as they had not been easily accessible prior to Massie's work. Her approach is largely empirical and less theoretically critical than Davin but she musters the evidence to refute Davin's case that the movement was 'an imperialist device to blame and control women in the interest of the future of the nation', especially as it was founded by social radicals. She suggests instead that 'the Centre operated through a women's network, with a nineteenth-century philanthropic base transmuted into the new philanthropy of the twentieth-century'. Early twentieth-century philanthropy was based on more sociological principles and was the forerunner to social work. She finds the leadership 'highly reminiscent' of the female groundbreakers of the nineteenth century: Florence Nightingale (1820-1910), Josephine Butler (1828-1906) and Elizabeth Garrett Anderson (1836-1917).

An influential figure in these debates was Dr Truby King (Sir Frederic Truby King 1858-1938). He was a New Zealander who started as a cattle breeder. He developed strong and radical medical interests in child health and mental health. He set up the 'Royal New Zealand Society for the Health of Mothers and Children', known as the Plunket Society and became Director of Child Health for New Zealand. He was treated as a national hero in New Zealand, knighted and given a state funeral.

King worked in the UK for some years and in 1918 he started the 'Babies of the Empire Society' and strongly influenced the 'Mothercraft Training Society' whose centre moved from Kensington to Cromwell House, 104 Highgate Hill (a Grade 1 listed seventeenth-century building, now occupied by the Ghanaian Embassy). They had bought this from the Great Ormond Street Hospital for Sick Children who for decades had used it as a convalescent home. The Mothercraft Training Society was largely for the training of experienced nurses (3-month course), midwives (6 months) and untrained women and girls (one year). It seems not to have had a focus on the poor and disadvantaged, and held a lofty view of 'the destiny of motherhood' for patriotic British women. The Society ceased to exist after 1952. Dr King was received at the Centre in the 1920s as a distinguished guest, but there seems to have been no close connection between the institutions. His ideas on child rearing, which involved a high degree of distance and non-tactile behaviour between mother and child, and well-spaced breast-feeding, became a leading orthodoxy in the UK from the 1930s to early 1950s. His ideas were impractical for the kind of working-class parents who attended the Manor Gardens Centre clinics.

The ground was virtually cut from under the eugenicists' feet after the appalling revelations of the experiments on humans encouraged by the German National Socialist Party and their racist policies. Since then the successors of the eugenics movement tend to be found among far right organisations. However new genetic research has revived some interest in genetic intervention in cases of incurable hereditary conditions. It remains an area of knotty problems for medical ethics, social morality and government policy.

Names and locations of the Centre

After a few months at the Presbyterian Mission in Elthorne Road and some space in the Upper Holloway Baptist Chapel in 1914, the Centre began to rent No. 9 Manor Gardens for £45 per annum subletting the basement to the London Invalid Kitchen. This space has been used as a kitchen, canteen and café ever since. A gift from the American Women's Club in London allowed us to extend to No. 8 in 1918 which was acquired with co-operation from Great Northern Hospital and the GPO. By 1920 further generosity from the AWC allowed us to move into Nos. 6 and 7 as wards for babies and their mothers. Planning permission for an extension was granted in 1925. The architect was Arthur Keen RIBA, younger brother of W.B. Keen. In 1928 the Duchess of York opened the building that links the two pairs of early semi-detached Victorian villas. These together with the 'laundry building' outhouse, (now known as the Dame Geraldine Hall, after its redevelopment with funds from her legacy), remain in our possession today. There was a plan and a seed fund to rebuild the old houses, but the economic crises of the 1930s and then the war prevented this happening. Nonetheless, demand for our services was such that at various times we established branches in Junction Road, Fonthill Road, Seven Sisters Road and Blythe Mansions in Hornsey Rise.

The Centre has changed its name several times over the years. It began as the North Islington School for Mothers, then the North Islington Maternity Centre. In 1923 it changed to North Islington Infant Welfare Centre and School for Mothers, reflecting a broader approach to the notion of 'welfare'. The term 'School for Mothers' was dropped as the Centre expanded its vision and role. In 1988 there were two registered charities: North Islington Welfare Centre and Manor Gardens Community

Trust. By 2004 we felt the need to drop 'North Islington' as our area of operations was by now borough-wide and beyond. The charity adopted our present name Manor Gardens Welfare Trust, Registered Charity No. 1063053. None of the other institutions in the road use the name Manor Gardens in their titles.

The Mothers and Fathers Committees

The Centre was led and managed by a General Committee chaired by Lady Crosfield, which soon had about 20 members. This included representatives from outside organisations. The Executive Committee of nine members was selected from the General Committee and chaired by Florence Keen. Meetings were frequent. In addition there were two parents' committees.

The Mothers Committee

In the 1920s and 30s the most important special committee was the Mothers Committee. Its greatest size was 26 members with an average attendance of 13-14. Florence Keen chaired the committee which consisted of young mothers who had brought their children to the clinics. The most practical and frequent tasks were organising groups to oversee the temporary storage of prams, and the serving of tea to visitors (strictly not to be given to children). But they could influence day-to-day practices and had a great many other activities. Chief of these was fund raising, by all sorts of means: collecting tins, sale of 'scent cards', holding bazaars and jumble sales (one raised £260), running a bookstall in Caledonian Market, organising dances, collecting clothes for 'necessitous mothers', and managing a 'community notice board' where messages could be left for one penny a week. They also organised sewing groups. They occasionally became involved in local issues as when they opposed the extension of a liquor licence. On the educational front they organised visits to local dairies (Manor Farm Dairy and United Dairies, Stroud Green).

The mothers were keen to learn and they proposed topics on which Florence Keen, Miss Davies the Superintendent and Dr Knox would speak. Precisely because the topics were often chosen by the mothers and reflect what they wanted to hear about, and no doubt the staff wanted them to learn about, it is interesting to list them. There were certainly many more than these.

Mrs Keen
Breast-feeding
Bronchitis and pneumonia
Care of the skin
Constipation of the bowels
Disease prevention
Discipline and punishment
Flies, clothes and milk
Harm and disfigurement done by dummies

Housekeeping on £3 per week
Household budgets
How to make the public aware of what the Centre exists for
National Savings
On tour in Italy and Sicily
Rheumatism in children
The washing of flannels [nappies]
Teeth
Vaccination for smallpox

Miss Davies
Diarrhoea
First aid and minor ailments
Influenza
Measles
Summer diet of toddlers
The value of antenatal clinics
Ventilation
Whooping cough

Dr Knox
Artificial sunlight
Burns, cramp and convulsions
Infectious diseases
The value of post-natal clinics

The Fathers Committee

The Fathers Committee is of considerable interest, if only for the fact that there was such a committee at all. Set up by 1922, this has to be seen in the context of the radical mood in Islington at the time, which gave rise to such jibes as 'Red Islington' and 'The Republic of Islington'. In 1923 the Fathers Committee held a debate on the future of voluntary welfare centres. The motion carried was as follows:

'That this meeting considers that in the best interests of society, Infant Welfare Centres should be established and organised by voluntary efforts, financially aided by the Ministry of Health and local authority, and that the work should co-operate and be co-ordinated with that of the local authority while retaining its freedom of action.'

This position statement is close to what the Centre has stood for since. It is interesting that the men were not attracted to the idea of municipalisation.

The Fathers Committee was one of the few committees not chaired by Mrs Keen. In 1926 the Fathers Committee, through the Conjoint Committee (see below) objected to a phrase used by other centres in Islington that 'those who could not afford to

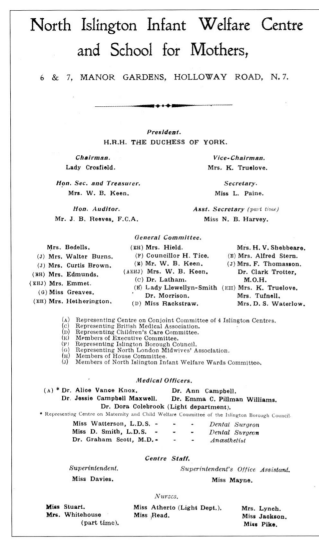

The Committee structure in 1926.

employ their own doctor should come to the Centre. They felt it contained a sting and that they were considered paupers for coming to the Centre'. In 1935 Mr H. H. Cross led a deputation from the Committee and read a paper at the Annual Conference of Maternity and Child Welfare Associations, the first time a father had given a paper to this conference. He was elected 'propaganda secretary' of the Central Union of Fathers Sections and in 1938 became Vice-President of this body.

The Fathers Committee was active in fundraising at events at the Centre and elsewhere in the borough. A notable occasion, in March 1934, was a dance in the Central Library; this was a Radio and Variety Show, at which the popular Western Brothers, Kenneth and George entertained in aid of the Centre.

The 'Conjoint Committee' [of Islington Centres]

Many sub-committees and ad hoc committees have come and gone and changed their shape. For example an entertainments committee was set up in 1917 and a junior committee in 1936, which lasted a short time as most members were called up for war service. Two other committees were the 'Conjoint Committee' and the more important Wards Committee.

The Conjoint Committee first met in December 1917. It brought together the four centres and gave them a collective voice. Three centres had been set up following the success of the Manor Gardens Centre in the North. These were in the South:

6 Clephane Road (off Essex Road); East: 21 (later 10) Drayton Park (off Holloway Road) and West: 42 Richmond Road (later Avenue) (Barnsbury). These Centres preceded by several years the well-endowed Mother and Child Welfare Centres built at public expense such as the Pine Street Clinic (1927), League Street (1929) and the Finsbury Health Centre (1938). A comparable leader in the field of voluntary health centres is the famous 'Peckham Health Centre' first established by Dr Williamson and Dr Pearse as a pilot project from 1926-29 and greatly expanded in 1934. It faltered during the war and closed in 1950 having been unable to fit in with the NHS. The Pioneer Health Foundation survives as an active advocate of the original ideas and approaches. The Peckham Experiment, whose archives are in the Wellcome Library, adopted an approach very similar to that of the Manor Gardens Centre which emphasised the importance of 'studying health and the means of producing and maintaining it' in order to balance the overwhelming medical orthodoxy that dealt with 'manifest and advanced diseases and disabilities'.

The Conjoint Committee met four times a year at rotating venues, two or more people representing each centre. Florence Keen and Dr Campbell were the most regular attenders despite the fact that Keen found the meetings 'too long, trivial and frequent'. They shared information on best practice and co-operated with the Islington Committee for the Welfare of Mothers. With Florence Keen's leadership they were instrumental in setting up the London Federation of Women's Centres. They were able to speak with a collective voice to the Council and for example to the producers of baby milk (Glaxo, Cow and Gate, Ambrosia, Almata) urging them to state on their tins the need for children also to have fresh fruit juice daily. They co-operated with Islington-wide flag days and other events such as Baby Week and Islington Health Week.

They were not always in agreement with their Council partners. For example in May 1936 the Council's Committee of Co-operation asked if the centre would co-operate in pointing out to mothers 'the dangers and the illegality of abortion either by drugs or instruments'. This was not followed up. The Ministry of Health and parliament in the 1920s and 1930s were generally not in favour of birth control. In 1929 the British Medical Association estimated that 16.2% of all pregnancies terminated in abortion.

The Northern Centre was always the dominant partner in this coalition. Quite apart from the leading part played by the Centre's representatives on the Conjoint Committee, the following figures underline the disparities:

1922 Grants (in pounds) to four Welfare Centres in Islington				
Centre	est. MoH grant	IBC grant	total	%
North	2,400	2,270	4,720	51.00%
South	800	741	1,541	16.75%
East	500	463	963	10.75%
West	1,058	926	1,984	21.00%
total	**4,808**	**4,400**	**9,208**	**100%**

SUCCESS STORY

The Wards Committee

The American Women's Club of London (AWC), formed in 1899, was a group of mainly wealthy women who were either expatriates or resident American or British women married to American men. Their addresses reveal their status: all the best streets of Mayfair, Kensington, Chelsea and some country houses. They had connections with the American Embassy and the American Red Cross and the worlds of commerce and finance.

The Centre was first approached by the AWC Infant Welfare Committee in July 1916 when they expressed concern to provide 'wards for cases of malnutrition'. This was before the United Sates joined in the war on the side of the Allies. By 7 March 1917 wards had been set up at Nos. 8-9 Manor Gardens with their help. The partnership was called at first 'The American Ward for Infant Welfare at the North Islington Maternity Welfare Centre'. It soon became known as 'The North Islington Welfare Centre Wards'. The wives of two successive American Ambassadors opened clinics. The AWC themselves set up and ran the North Islington Wards Committee with representation from the Centre. Keen and Crosfield attended very regularly. For some twenty years or more the Wards Committee met about once every six to eight weeks. The Committee considered reports on the welfare of babies and mothers, on staff and on developments generally. A major concern was fund raising, which we shall discuss later. The Wards Committee had a budget that was distinct from the General Committee of the Centre but funds raised and income received from public authorities were shared between 'Centre' and 'Wards'.

There were soon several wards with a total of 18 beds or cots, six of them with additional accommodation for mothers. The average number of babies in the wards each year from 1921-39 was 139 (1921-29: 118; 1930-39: 157). The average length of stay was about one month in a range from one night to six months. The wards were obliged to close at the outbreak of war in 1939, but remained in partial use as day observation clinics.

The Wards Committee was run entirely by women, with a small core of dedicated supporters and prime movers:

Mrs Walter Burns	Chairman	1920-40
Mrs Arthur James	Committee	"
(godmother to the Duchess of York)		
Mrs Robert Emmet (major donor, £1,500)	" "	"
Mrs Curtis Brown	" "	"
Lady Domini Crosfield (MGC)	" "	"
Mrs Florence (WB) Keen (MGC)	" "	"

other long serving committee members
Mrs John Mulholland
Lady Carew-Pole
The Hon. Mrs Baring

SUCCESS STORY

Hon. Mrs Jenkinson
Mrs Horlick
Miss Raphael

other major donors
Mrs Franklyn Thomasson (& Col Thommason) donors (£1,500)
Mrs Nancy (William B.) Leeds (£100)

other income (from AWC related sources)
AWC Philanthropic Committee 1918 (£50)
American Red Cross 1918 (£500)
annual social events (see section below on fundraising)

Volunteers

The volunteers who helped the Centre included the Americans, the Highgate élite, prominent Islington citizens, the parents of children, local workers and others. All contributed time and money generously relative to their wealth and income. By 1915 there were 21 volunteer helpers with consultation in the clinics and 22 volunteer home visitors (including Mrs Hobhouse). In addition there were five volunteers with secretarial duties.

Volunteer workers have always been at the heart of the Centre and their work has been highly appreciated. In 1923 Florence Keen wrote of 'the splendid band of volunteer workers, who are always ready to enter into [the mothers'] troubles and help them to meet them'. Volunteering has been seen as part of community co-operation in the widest sense. In 1933 Florence Keen wrote:

'The keynote of the North Islington Centre is co-operation. One of the aims of the Centre is to attract as many friends as possible to come to our help, for the good of the North Islington community.'

Many volunteers were also members of the staff and management as we have begun to see. However the Centre paid wages to several key staff: the Superintendent Nurse and her assistant and other nurses. The Medical Officers gave their time free in the early days and often thereafter. The cook, laundry staff and the 'handyman' (janitor) were also waged.

People who attended the Centre

We have seen that some of those who visited and made use of the services of the Centre sometimes joined in the work as volunteers, whether as members of Mothers or Fathers Committees or in other working parties and activity circles. The people who came to Manor Gardens did so voluntarily. They were seldom referred to as 'patients', just mothers, babies and children, or families, and by personal name. Nowadays the rather impersonal term 'service user' is common; in some contexts

Mothers and young children in the garden in the 1920s.

terms such as 'beneficiaries' or even 'clientele' might be appropriate.

The personal and health records of the families are not yet accessible under the Data Protection Act. But we do have details of attendances and anecdotal reference. One source of great interest is the lists of occupations of fathers which were entered on the registration cards and in many years reported in the annual reports. They give a good idea of the kind of families who came even if they are not systematic samples. We must bear in mind that there was a regular turnover in users of the Centre. It was rather more likely that mothers would come with their first children; some would return with succeeding children; others might have absorbed what there was to learn and gained in confidence and satisfaction. Some families moved and in the 1920s and 1930s there was frequent 'slum clearance', especially from the south of the borough and the Borough of Finsbury. People came to live in LBI and LCC flats in the north and many families moved out of the north into housing estates in the suburbs. This continually reinforced the need for parent education. The turnover in local population took on a different character from the 1950s with considerable new migration from overseas, which will be discussed later.

Another stage was after 1970 as old housing was demolished or renewed. The population reached its lowest level in the 1980s when the combined populations of Islington and old Finsbury was some 40% of that of Islington alone in 1913.

The mothers who came lived in a circle round the Centre that we could describe as having a radius that was the distance a mother could push her pram there and back with a toddler or two or more. This was reckoned to be about a half-mile radius. This would have described an area that extended to Tube stations at Archway,

Nurses with young children in the garden in the 1920s.

Tufnell Park, Holloway Road and Finsbury Park *(see 1894 map on pp 10-11)*. Only some 3-4% of mothers came from neighbouring boroughs, which in places are not far away. A special category of users of the Centre were the mothers with babies in Holloway Women's Prison. At one time there were 32 prison babies for whom the Centre supplied dried milk, orange juice and cod liver oil.

In 1923 the occupations of 2,501 fathers were recorded, one of the largest samples. They include 118 job descriptions, from which we might derive the following approximate categories:

Blue collar workers	70.50%
White collar workers	13.50
Unemployed	8.50
Artisans	4.00
Uniformed public servants (of lowest ranks)	2.75
Pensioners	1.00
Of the blue collar workers:	
General labourers (unskilled and semi-skilled)	25%
Transport, communications and warehousing	30
Building and related trades	10
Engineering and metalworking	10
Others	25

Mothers waiting to go into the clinic, 1920s.

Of the 'general labourers' only 15% were 'factory hands'. In the category 'uniformed public servants' there were police (37), armed forces (21), and fire-fighters (10). Some less usual occupations were: piano manufacturers (34), tennis racquet makers (4), toy makers (4), silk embroiderers (3), billiard makers (2), lamplighter (1) and acrobat (1). These occupations reflect the local catchment area where there were no large factories and many small workshops. Many worked in public transport and local government offices as well as a great variety of shop-workers, services, provisions and catering. The figures for unemployment changed with the economic ups and downs of the times.

The great majority of fathers and their families might be termed 'working- class' and most of these probably identified themselves as such. This could even be the case in the few instances of jobs that are not working-class by definition such as junior schoolteacher. Clerks, while being white-collar workers, were poorly paid and by origin also could be included in the working-class category. On the other hand it is in the nature of so-called British 'class culture' that some people with aspirations like to 'identify up' as lower-middle or even middle-class. It is difficult to be precise in the absence of first hand social anthropological data. At the same time some people with jobs that can be described as 'respectable' may have been employed part-time. It is likely that more than half those attending were 'poor' or 'very poor' in Mayhew's terms, struggling to make ends meet. Many of the others would be in the category 'nearly poor' and a few just in the 'comfortable' zone.

SUCCESS STORY

'About a pound a week' was for long a popular gauge of poor people's budget, or perhaps it was what was left over for mothers after deductions by the male wage earner. Even as late as 1931 the Centre estimated that a minimum for a family of two parents and two children was £2 per week, or £1.10 shillings if the husband was working part time. A great many jobs paid less than £1.10 shillings per week, so most lived below any notion of a 'poverty line'. Florence Keen did on one occasion give a talk on a household budget of £3 per week. Perhaps she was trying to demonstrate what might really be necessary.

A letter from a mother to Nurse Davies in 1935 is evocative in this respect (original spelling and punctuation):

'I am very sorry I could not come any more to my dinners But my husband has got a new job. The salary is £3. 5 shillings a week and I feel that their is some other Mother would be glad of a good Dinner the same as I did when I had nothing hoping you will see my reason for not coming.'

Another strong British cultural trait has been for people to resist being called paupers, to be stigmatised as being dependent, possibly only able to survive by accepting life in a Workhouse. The stigma even shades into the use by others of the term 'poor' itself. One way of overcoming this was for the Centre to charge a very small sum for each attendance at a clinic. For twenty years this was fixed at one half penny; then in 1933 it was raised to one penny. For those who could not pay, a benevolent fund ensured that all who needed help received it. Some mothers could also donate a little more, usually just copper coins, and even insisted that there were collecting tins in the office and at talks. No doubt many small donations were made out of gratitude.

In its first week of operation in December 1913 nine mothers came to see the doctor at the Centre. By the end of the following year 70-80 visitors per week were said to have come, maybe some 3,500 or more in the year. Numbers steadily increased during the war and grew fast just afterwards to 12,978 visitors in 1919-20 and tripling to 37,000 by 1926-7. In that year the total included 20,865 registered babies and 1,181 expectant mothers. In addition 1,455 people attended the Dental Clinic for the children. In the same year Centre staff and volunteers made 13,545 visits to the homes of mothers.

Visitors to the Centre

The Centre was a busy and bustling place. It received a great many visitors who came to inspect, to learn and compare notes. Donors were always welcome to visit the work. School children came to gain an insight into the work of the Centre, and at times there were trainees receiving dedicated instruction.

One important category of visitor was that of professionals and people of high social and political rank from overseas. We know that the Keen and Crosfield families were cosmopolitans, even internationalists, with many friends and connections in

A visit by the Queen of Spain in 1919.

An Indian delegation in 1933.

Europe and beyond. An early visitor was the Queen of Spain in 1919. She was Victoria Eugenie of Battenberg, wife of King Alfonso XIII of Spain, a granddaughter of Queen Victoria and first cousin to King George V. In 1922 Prince Mahidol Adulyadej (1892-1927), Prince of Siam, son of King Chulalongkorn (Rama V) visited the Centre. He had studied medicine at Harvard University in the USA and continued his studies in Edinburgh. His first child Princess Galayani Vadhana was born in London in 1925. He was the father of the present reigning monarch of Thailand King Bhumibol Adulyadej. Although he died young from an incurable condition, his achievements in his home country were already such that he is known as 'the Father of Thai Medicine'. Not long after his visit a Thai student, Miss Varavan, came to study at the Centre.

Lady Irwin, a friend of the Centre and wife of the 30th Viceroy of India (1926-31), later Lord Halifax, Foreign Secretary (1938-40), brought a group of distinguished Indian ladies and some Bengali Parsee gentlemen. The latter were delighted by the sunlight treatment which they recognised as part of their own very ancient wisdom. A more contro-versial figure was Dr Truby King whom we have already discussed. Distinguished visitors after the Second World War included Arch-bishop Huddleston (of whom more later) and Margery Fry, a Quaker and prison reformer who gave a talk at the Centre. She was the first Director of the Howard League for Penal Reform and Principal of Somerville College, Oxford.

A partial list of some of the countries from which our visitors came over the first fifty years includes the following:

Prince Mahidol, 'Father of Thai Medicine', 1922.

Europe
Austria, Belgium, Bulgaria, Cyprus, Czechoslovakia, Denmark, Estonia, France, Germany, Greece, Iceland, Italy, Lithuania, Norway, Poland, Russia, Spain, Sweden, Switzerland

Asia
Bangladesh, Burma, Ceylon, China, Hong Kong, India, Indonesia, Israel, Japan, Korea, Lebanon, Malaysia, Pakistan, Palestine, Singapore, Taiwan, Thailand

Africa
Ghana, Nigeria, Sierra Leone, Rhodesia, South Africa, Zanzibar

Americas
Brazil, British Guiana, British Honduras, Canada, Chile, Jamaica, Mexico, USA

Australasia
Australia, New Zealand

Domini Crosfield, Florence Keen and Dr Jessie Campbell (later Lady Maxwell) made many trips abroad, often in each other's company, especially to the European countries. Domini Crosfield also visited South America and the USA. They gave talks about their travels on their return. They were particularly impressed by the arrangements for infant welfare in Austria. One notable visit was made by Domini Crosfield and her friend Madame Venizelos, wife of the republican Greek Prime Minister, to Czechoslovakia, where they met Thomas Masaryk (1850-1937) leader of the Czech independence movement from 1907 and founder and President of the Czech Republic (1918-35).

Services provided 1913-40

Mothers brought their babies to the Centre because they were concerned for their health. If they came with seriously ill babies they would be referred to the Great Northern Hospital, just round the corner, or another hospital nearer their home. They were asked to register and this required answering a short questionnaire administered by a doctor or a competent volunteer. An early version of this is given as an appendix. It recorded the mother's history of childbirth and method of feeding. Dr Maxwell tells us that 'The consultation began, not with "how many children have you got?" but with "how many children have you lost?"' Of note are the questions about the parents, their health, employment and housing. Children's diseases are listed as measles, whooping cough, scarlet fever, chicken pox, diphtheria and 'other'.

Dr Maxwell later recalled the prevalence of lice and fleas in the waiting areas and the swirling dust caused by the women's long skirts. Ursula Carter (née Keen),

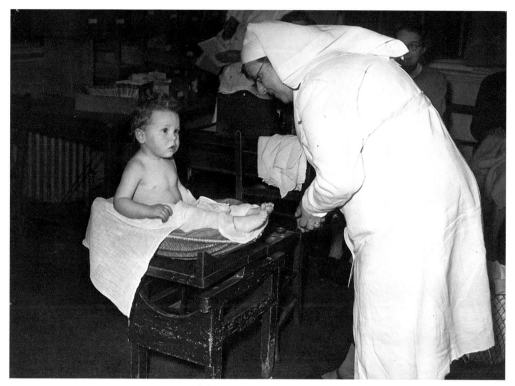

Baby weighing in the 1920s.

who spent some time as an intern trainee nurse remembered how she had to scrub up and delouse carefully when she got home at night.

Once this form of triage was complete the baby was examined and weighed. The mother was offered various kinds of advice, encouragement and support. A home visit might be appropriate to assess the family circumstances and advise on the spot. Appalling conditions were met with. In one instance a small child had been strapped into a high chair for much of the time and had not been able to learn to walk. Diet was of the greatest importance. Anecdotes about babies being given sponge cake at one month and pork pie and eels by nine months are probably not much exaggerated. Breast-feeding was encouraged and 'valves' (breast pumps), bottles and teats were offered at cost or possibly free. Special baby food supplements were dispensed by qualified volunteers. These foods and medicines included generic products such as cod liver oil and petroleum emulsion, and branded products such as Maltene and Marylebone cream. Toothbrushes were also available. It is not entirely clear which items might be offered free of charge. The usual formula was that at least a token payment would be asked. But if the mother was very poor the Benevolent Fund might pay the cost. At the most, a well-discounted price was paid. In a similar way helpers at the Centre might be a mixture of unpaid voluntary workers, paid volunteers (e.g. 3 pence an hour for making up simple baby garments)

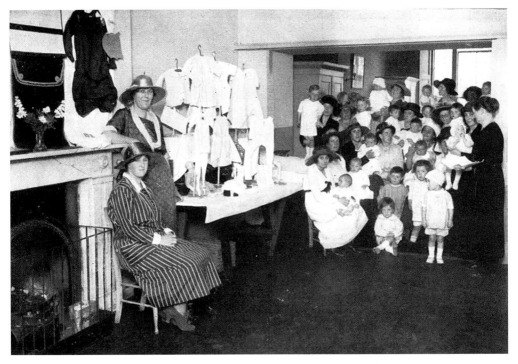

The Assembly Room with a display of baby clothes 1920s.

and paid workers (often part-time). Among the latter were home helps who in 1915 received twelve shillings and sixpence a week plus a wartime bonus of two shillings and sixpence.

Baby clothing was discussed and advice and materials given out or sold at cost. Classes were held in cutting out and sewing simple items. The aim was to encourage affordable clothing that was hygienic, easy to clean and allowed freedom of movement in contrast to the old custom of 'swaddling' the baby tightly. Forty years after she arrived at the Centre Dr Jessie Campbell (MB, CHB, DPH) and by now Lady Maxwell, gave a talk at the Centre's AGM on 27 September 1955. Her amusing, and horrifying, recollection of baby clothes is worth looking at in full.

'By the voluntary worker sat our one Health Visitor who undressed and weighed the babies. The young mothers of today have no idea of what dressing and undressing the baby meant in those days (1914). First, there was the binder – the last remnant of the swaddling clothes – the battle of the binder was waged for many years. The binder had to be carefully unstitched and the Health Visitor had always to have a needle and cotton ready to stitch it on again – a most unnerving procedure. Next, there was a double-breasted vest with many tapes fastened on the front. Next, a long flannel garment called a Barrie (why, I don't know, it's not in the Oxford Dictionary; but in a Scotch Dictionary I found it described as part of the swaddling clothes). This was also double-breasted (four layers already on the baby's

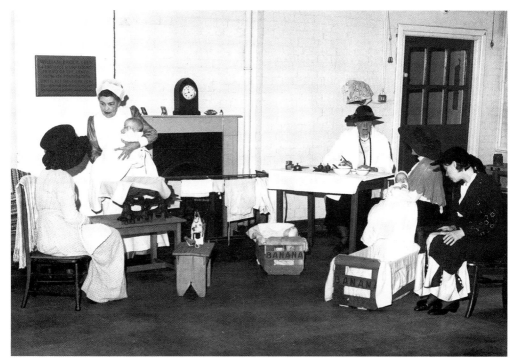

Banana crates were in demand for making cots. This photograph is from about 1942 as it has a plaque in honour to W.B. Keen who died in 1941.

chest) and had slits through which you passed tapes, and it was fastened at the back. Next, a long white cotton petticoat - good hardwearing cotton – fastened at the back. Next, and lastly, a frock of cotton, or more commonly, flannelette – pink for a girl and blue for a boy – and this, to use once again the monotonous refrain, fastened at the back and tied like a sash. The poor infant was turned round and round in the process of this "Operation Dressing and Undressing"! I am not forgetting the many nappies, especially the thick flannel pilch that scented the whole Hall! I don't believe the word pilch is ever used today! But it is in the Oxford Dictionary and has strange meanings, one of which is a flannel napkin. All these garments were about twelve inches longer than their occupants.'

Cots and bedclothes were another issue. The Centre was known for its re-use of banana crates as cots and regularly appealed for the donation of them. In wartime they must have been scarce. They were still in use in 1942. The crates or boxes were sandpapered and creosoted. A hammock of unbleached calico was sewn in and pillows made from old sheets and shirts. Cut-down blankets were secured with safety pins and if possible a more decorative coverlet went on top.

By 1918 the Borough Council began to pay for free milk for babies and expectant and nursing mothers. The range of services on offer increased year by year. Post-natal clinics were soon followed by antenatal clinics. Mothers were lent scales for seven days at a time, and fathers are reported as being keen on recording the babies'

Mothers exercising in the 1920s.

Sunlight treatment in 1948.

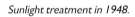

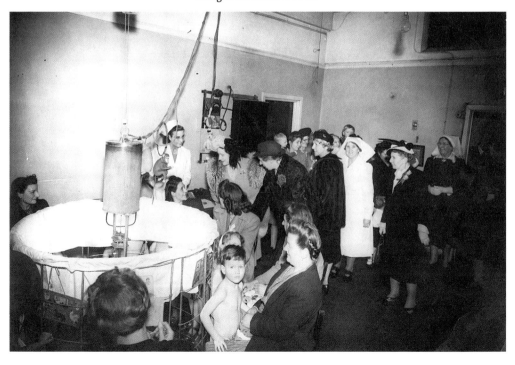

weight. Cookery lessons and sewing classes started early on.

As the wards developed some babies could be kept under close care and examination for several days or weeks. An example from the first year, in 1916, is of a baby of a few weeks who was admitted weighing three pounds after losing weight since birth. After 2-3 weeks at the clinic he returned home, improving. One ward allowed mothers to stay with their babies, often a necessary form of respite. Home helps for the period of confinement were organised.

The public health services offered little support for mothers and children under school age of five. Increasingly the Centre became concerned with the 'toddlers' aged 1-4 years and expanded services accordingly. One of these was the art and technique of massage. This was started in 1917 and by 1923 there were massage sessions on three days a week. In 1933 there were three volunteer masseuses and 1,316 people used this service.

One of the most pioneering contributions was the introduction in 1924 of sunlight treatment using the Eidenov Carbon Arc Light recommended by Professor Leonard Hull of the Medical Research Institute. There were daily clinics for the treatment of rickets especially but also for general muscle tone and catarrh. It was also found beneficial in treating depression in mothers. Rickets was one of the worst scourges of the early twentieth century. Sunlight and a good diet (green vegetables, milk and Vitamin C) were the chief means of prevention and cure. Bad urban housing and atmosphere were major enemies. Cities had about one-sixth the sunlight of rural areas due to air pollution. It comes as no surprise to learn that Glasgow had the worst figures for rickets, and that the condition was unknown in Italy.

Fundraising

The landscape of public health provision changed out of all recognition during the twentieth century and the Centre was part of that history. At the beginning of the century private philanthropy was the primary source of funding for health care. Public Health measures were introduced in a patchwork manner over the first fifty years or so until the introduction of the National Health Service in 1948. Before this, state management powers were given to local authorities, in this case to the London Boroughs and later to the London County Council (LCC). The Ministry of Health was not established until 1919. As we have seen the health needs of mothers and babies received a small share at first. There is no question but that voluntary institutions, such as the Centre, were responsible for leading the way and encouraging these measures at a higher and national level.

The tennis parties at *Witanhurst* were one of our most reliable sources of funding for some 35 years. They were either 'American Tournaments' competitions, for which there was an entry fee of £1.10s or Exhibition Matches for which there was an entrance fee and a programme, sold to raise money. Arthur Crosfield is usually thanked for 'providing refreshments'. These events were held in the week after Wimbledon when famous international tennis players would stay on at Domini's request. On the last occasion in 1960 the event was rained off – the only mention of such an occurrence

Domini Crosfield and Wimbledon champion, Fred Perry, at Witanhurst in 1934.

– and Domini arranged for an adept Yogi to entertain and instruct her guests, who were fascinated by the demonstration. Yoga was relatively unknown at the time and may have been introduced to her by her good friend, and Highgate neighbour, Yehudi Menuhin.

The tennis stars included Wimbledon finalists and winners from many countries: Suzanne Lenglen of France, who between 1919-25 had more wins than any player before Martina Navratilova, Jean Booth (France, between 1922-39), Renée Lacoste (France), Fred Perry (UK, 1934, 1935 and 1936), Bunny Austin (UK, finalist in 1932 and 1938) and Jean Borotra (France, 1922-39, winner in 1924, and 1948-64). After the war they included Louise Brough (USA, winner 1948-50 and 1955) and Maureen Connolly (USA, 1952-4).

So for the first fifty years of the Centre, the work was crucially supported by private philanthropic donations, charitable giving in cash or kind by individuals, and a few businesses and charitable foundations. The proportion of the Centre's income that came from government and local government sources increased steadily and despite its independence from the NHS – which we shall discuss later. Statutory funding has now become the preponderant contribution to our funding.

It is a commonplace of fundraising strategy that you try at first to engage a small number of high profile wealthy people who are willing to set the tone and

AN AMERICAN LAWN TENNIS

TOURNAMENT

IN AID OF

North Islington Infant Welfare Wards

WILL BE HELD ON

TUESDAY, JULY 17th.,

AND

THURSDAY, JULY 19th

LADIES' DOUBLES - 11 a.m. - 1 p.m.

MIXED DOUBLES - 5.30 p.m. - 7.30 p.m.

TICKETS—£1 each for one event,

or 30/- for both events from

Hon. Secs. : HON. MRS. MULHOLLAND,

20, CLEVELAND SQUARE, W. 2.

PADDINGTON 0221.

and MISS DIANA HORNBY,

SHELLEY HOUSE, CHELSEA EMBANKMENT.

KENSINGTON 2543.

1ST & 2ND PRIZES

Entries close July 13th, 1928.

Invitation to a tennis tournament held at Witanhurst on behalf of Manor Gardens in 1928.

lead the way. But alas, Manor Gardens Centre has never had one great benefactor. The manner of our establishment contained a flaw, one could say, that continues to affect our resources and capabilities. We have never had any endowments or capital reserves for investment. Simply put, this means we have had to live a fairly hand-to-mouth existence for a hundred years. There have been few guarantees of continuity. This is a situation that calls for urgent redress at the beginning of our second century. The Keen and Crosfield families, through their unpaid work, their own donations and their fundraising activities, were the most significant elements in maintaining the Centre. Their circles of friends and friends of those friends made up most of the other significant supporters. The Keen family had at times at least five members subscribing personally and several other families had two to four subscribing members. There was always a core of faithful donors who included most of the senior staff and volunteers at the Centre and a cluster of socially prominent names.

We started on a very small scale indeed and very optimistically. Our first year expenditure was £125.11.11. We had 78 committed annual subscribers by 1915 including three who donated £2 and over and eighteen at £1 and over. It seems to have been fashionable to give sums in guineas (one pound and one shilling) which were much used in such less commercial transactions as philanthropy, professional fees and gambling. There are also 43 people separately listed as (one-off) donors. Some gave in both categories, such as Mrs Ada Wallas who subscribed for £1.1 and donated £5. Viscountess Wolmar pledged £10 if four others would do the same.

They did, including Mrs Tufnell from a longstanding North Islington (Tufnell Park) family, and a member of the General Committee. Lady Islington donated £5.

Since the following section is going to refer rather often to sums of money it may help to use an approximate multiplier figure of x50 in order to reach an approximation to today's values. Occasionally a figure of x70 has been used by others, so these comparisons are likely to be conservative. This does not work for many things (e.g. house prices) but seems to work reasonably well for charitable giving. Inflation remained low until the late 1950s. Thus we could use the following conversions as a rough guide:

1913-1938	2013
1 shilling	£2.50
£1	£50
£2	£100
£5	£250
£10	£500
£20	£1,000
£100	£5,000
£500	£25,000
£1,000	£50,000
£5,000	£250,000
£10,000	£500,000
£20,000	£1,000,000

Any gift great or small was the usual slogan, but subscriptions were invited from one shilling annually. Sums of £2-3 were standard from our Royal Patron, which would have been considered a respectable amount from people with a broad portfolio of causes to support. The building appeal from 1924 was more ambitious, stating that 'One friend has promised £100 if nine others would do the same'. Some subscribers stayed the course longer than others. By 1916 there was a magnificent total of 425 subscribers and donors. Numbers fluctuated, dropping to 156 in 1934 after three years in which the annual reports record growing poverty, with middle and upper classes also affected..

The Annual Report for 1921 is a good instance of the early days when charitable income still exceeded local or central government support.

1920/21	voluntary and charitable income (pounds shillings and pence)	
	dance at *Witanhurst* (Crosfield)	£1,036.6.10
	sale of work at *Mayfield* (Keen)	525.17.3
	jumble sale	59.16.3
	City Parochial Fund	40.0.0
	North London Collegiate School	6.17.6

	total voluntary & charitable	£1,668.17.10	
1920/21	London Borough of Islington	£1,580.00.00	

For the year 1926/27 when the new building project was started the MoH contributed £9,865 and the Centre raised £6,724 towards an estimated total cost of £17,480 for the freehold, new building and refurbishment of the old buildings. The final total needed was £19,903 to include bank interest on a partial loan and completion costs. So the Centre managed to raise over one-third of the total cost. The final amount was paid for by a mortgage for £3,125 with the Alliance Assurance Society payable over 25 years. The trustees responsible at the time were Sir Arthur Henry Crosfield, Mr William Brock Keen and Mr Roger Hetherington (a civil engineer).

Although the Centre has never received gifts in the highest echelons of munificence, there have been some notable individual donations:

1916	£650	anonymous donor
1963	£1,000	legacy of Mme Venizelou
1972	£14,627	legacy of Mrs Annie Brant of Chicago, aunt of the late Dr Eve Atkins who had served as a medical doctor at the Centre, died 1963
1986	£31,106	legacy of Dame Geraldine Aves (1898-1986) Chairman 1977-1981

Our most regular and loyal supporters, among them especially the Crosfield and Keen families, have contributed, in total, sums as great as these over the years.

A wide range of charitable foundations has helped us, some from the earliest days. They include the City Bridge Trust Fund, the City Parochial Fund (now known as the Trust for London), Nuffield and most notably the King's Fund (formerly known as King Edward's Hospital Fund for London).

The BBC began by giving us airtime for public appeals in the 1930s, one of which was made by Domini Crosfield. These tended to yield quite modest sums. More recently BBC's Children in Need programmes and campaigns have yielded more substantial support. The BBC filmed for six days at Manor Gardens in 1977 for which we received a fee.

One interesting charitable group was the members of the Stock Exchange Amateur Dramatic Association. They produced an annual magazine called *Help Yourself* which organisations such as the Manor Gardens Centre could sell for their own benefit. For some ten years in the 1920s and 30s this raised a useful amount, reaching £1,723 in the year 1931. Of course this required a lot of volunteer work by the Centre's friends to make it such a success.

Next in importance to our voluntary income from donations and subscriptions and charitable foundations has been what we can broadly term 'Entertainments'.

Of these by far the most important were the tennis parties and garden parties at *Witanhurst* and *Mayfield*. These were annual events for more than fifty years, bar a few in the Second World War. Net receipts (no pun intended) to the Centre were often in the order of £500 or so per annum.

Other major forms of entertainment were organised by the American Women's Club of London (AWC) who had their own entertainments committee. The most public events were grand balls and dances, though the income from these was seldom spectacular relative to the effort and outlay. For some of the larger events it was usual to employ a professional organiser. For example one was paid a fee of 50 guineas to organise one of the Crosfield tennis parties, another £166 for a 'Lucky Ball' at the Hyde Park Hotel in 1929 attended by the Duke of York, the future King George VI, and his wife Duchess of York who was our Patron. Other notable dances and balls were one held at the country home of Mrs Arthur James in North Mymms and a 'Servants' Ball' held in the home of Viscount and Lady Clifden at 37 Grosvenor Square, for which 600 tickets were sold and 400 attended. One of the most fun it seems was an April Fool's Day dance at the American Women's Club organised by the younger members; music was by the Cambridge University Footlights Band; Jack Hulton and Cicely Courtneidge performed, and the well-known cartoonist of the day 'Fougasse' gave an original drawing for *Punch* magazine to be auctioned. Musical concerts were also held. Miss Ruth Draper, an American singer, gave concerts before and after the Second World War. In 1928 she raised £410 for which a baby cot was named after her. Miss Otis Skinner, a musician who performed for charity, was another regular contributor.

Reflecting the upper-class pastimes of the day the AWC put on a range of highly successful events such Bridge and Whist tournaments, Backgammon, and an extraordinary Mah Jong competition held at Claridges, raising £110. This was all 'top of the market' outreach and no doubt helped raise the profile of the Centre and the Wards generally and brought in additional donations.

But in between Mayfair and Highgate village, so to say, there lay the whole of Islington. It seems few potential partners were not involved in some way or other. The most financially rewarding for some years was the Islington cinemas' contribution, including the Holloway Odeon from the first year of its opening in 1938. This was under a London-wide 'Sunday Cinematographic Entertainments' scheme whereby the cinemas gave 25% of Sunday takings to selected charities. Other Islington wide fundraising included various 'flag days'.

Educational institutions have always been counted as valued partners. Children of local primary schools, such as Grafton, Montem, Yerbury and Duncombe, some of whom had come to the Centre as babies, held small entertainments or made things for sale. The private schools to the north, Channing Girls' School, Highgate Boys' School (later Boys and Girls) and North London Collegiate School were generous in their support with cash collections and goods for sale. They also sent senior girls to visit the Centre as part of their syllabus. The Northern Polytechnic (now London Metropolitan University) on Holloway Road organised a dramatic performance to raise money for the Centre. The Little Angel Puppet Theatre helped in a similar way. Today, of course, many of our former supporters are themselves trying to raise funds for their own purposes and for survival.

The Centre itself staged modest musical and theatrical performances in the Princess Elizabeth Hall. It also regularly held sales of various kinds: sales of work, clothing sales ('Make do and Mend'), jumble sales, rummage sales, white elephant sales and bazaars. Mothers ran a bookstall at Caledonian Market. The Fathers Committee did their bit, once putting on a dance competition in the Town Hall. The 1,200 or so workers in the GPO building, of whom 1,100 were women, were good customers and contributors. They made an annual cash collection for us, and several of their number acted as volunteers for the Centre at the end of their working day. Two notable examples were Miss Dodds and Miss Obard who for many years were familiar figures at the Centre changing and feeding the babies. Others contributed advanced clerical and statistical skills.

At the micro end of the scale our dedicated supporters, mothers and fathers, did their best to make sure everyone had a chance to give something. They collected silver paper, organised a farthing collection in 1923, a penny collection in 1916 and 'a mile of pennies' in 1932. These sums of course were not quite so petty as one might think. A penny could buy a bus fare or some sweets, or a bun. A farthing was a quarter of a penny so you might have to save up for a bun, but a mile of pennies laid side by side might be worth about £250 (or £3,000 if stacked up!).

Many gifts were made in kind and most of them saved us considerable sums of money that are hard to estimate. For some years the annual reports give a wish list of needed items, including in 1916 'toys, mangle or wringer, banana crates, coal, nursery chairs'. Well-wishers donated a gramophone and a radio for the nurses and other staff and visitors. They were doubtless well used at the regular Christmas lunches for which the senior ladies would offer a goose, a turkey, puddings and fruit. The most significant in terms of equivalent cash value was the gift of time and knowledge however expert or everyday. We can begin to get some idea of the value by adding up the salaries and fees we now pay to our core staff, our accountant, lawyer, architect and fundraising consultant. All of these services were provided free of cost for most of our first half-century.

Other useful gifts in kind were made by local retailers. Among our many suppliers of those for whom we have records, we know that Jones Brothers and Boots the Chemist, both on Holloway Road, made contributions. Free advertisement of the Crosfield tennis events was offered by *Tennis Weekly*. Our predecessors were very adept at making use of the Press to place letters and features about our work. Other local shops and tradesmen gave free or discounted food and groceries (tea, flour, oats), coal, furnishing material and floor coverings. Even more local would be the gifts of second hand items: clothes, toys, bric-a-brac, and banana crates. Gifts from further afield included pieces of new cloth from the St Mary's Needlewomen's Guild, used gramophone records from the BBC, corn flour and 'Swiss Milk' (tinned) from the Queensland Association. In addition to regular cash subscriptions, our

Royal Patron and her daughters as children made delightful occasional gifts such as boxes of honey from Argentina and tickets to Whipsnade Zoo. We received gifts of unspecified surgical equipment and a somewhat mysterious gift of an Aga cooker, which apparently the cook did not like.

Whenever an opportunity has presented itself the Centre has given recognition to important donors. We recognise and thank all donors 'great and small' but here we refer to exceptional acts of generosity. The most common has been to name buildings, rooms and other facilities after them. The contribution of HRH the late Queen Mother is reflected in the naming of the Princess Elizabeth Hall after her daughter, now HM Queen Elizabeth II. Florence Keen's name is attached to our premises in the Beaux Arts Building (formerly GPO and No. 10 Manor Gardens). Dame Geraldine Aves is remembered in the Dame Geraldine Hall. Cots in the Wards and a surgery room were named after their donors or dedicated to people of the donor's choice. Unfortunately nothing is permanent and some dedications have lapsed when the functions they served have been discontinued. Oddly there is no specific lasting memorial to Domini, Lady Crosfield. It is our intention to renew these traditions.

This section has been about contributions from private individuals and the 'voluntary sector' as we now call it. The value of subventions and contracts from local and government authorities will become clearer as our story progresses. It should be said here that the Centre's reputation and therefore its ability to raise money from both private and voluntary, and public and statutory sectors has always depended on our maintenance of excellent relations with the public sector. We have stressed our independence and been fearless in voicing criticism when we have thought it appropriate and for the public good. We have practised the greatest transparency and our Annual Reports are a good example of this. Moreover we have always been open to inspection by health and educational authorities, the Ministry of Health, the Borough, the King's Fund and other agencies. We have welcomed visitors to learn for themselves what we do. In the end it has been the high standards we have set ourselves that have ensured our continuing good reputation and success.

Royal Patronage
Manor Gardens Centre has been privileged to have two Royal Patrons, Princess Christian and Elizabeth, Duchess of York, later the Queen Mother.

Princess Christian 1916-1923
Princess Christian (1846-1923) was baptised Helena. She was the third daughter, and fifth child, of Queen Victoria. She married Prince Christian of Schleswig-Holstein in 1866. Her husband died in 1917. Her son Albert, Duke of Schleswig-Holstein, was in the Prussian army during the war but vowed nonetheless not to fight against his 'motherland'.

Princess Christian was a woman of great intelligence and many talents. She is said to have had 'a good head for business'. She was Queen Victoria's personal secretary until the Queen died. She played the piano with Charles Hallé. She was a gifted translator, artist and needlewomen, founding the Royal School of Needlework in 1876. Her greatest interest was in nursing and the welfare of children. She was a founding member of the British Red Cross and founding President of the Royal British Nurses Association in 1887, a predecessor of the Royal College of Nursing. In addition to campaigning on behalf of nurses she showed concern for the unemployed and actively supported women's rights, to her mother's disapproval. All her talents and interests would have appealed greatly to Florence Keen and Domini Crosfield, and would have been of practical value to the Centre.

She was sidelined by the new court on King Edward's accession in 1901, but remained a popular figure. She continued her public work, and in 1916 consented to become our first Patron. It was in 1917 that the British royal family changed its surname from Saxe-Coburg and Gotha to Windsor. She was most likely invited by Domini Crosfield who was known for her work for the Red Cross by this time, and for which she was later to receive the gold medal of honour of the Royal Red Cross (RRC). Princess Christian remained our Royal Patron until her death on 9 June 1923, aged 77. Her niece Princess Alice, Countess of Athlone (1884-1981) was a long-standing friend and correspondent of Domini Crosfield.

The Duchess of York (later Queen Elizabeth and Elizabeth the Queen Mother) 1923-2002

Our second Royal Patron was Elizabeth, Duchess of York (née Bowes-Lyon). She was a friend of Lady Domini Crosfield, our Chairman from 1919-1959, and others in her social and tennis playing circles before she married the Duke of York in 1923. She became our Patron later that year. She had lost a brother in the First World War. She was of a Scottish noble family and so strictly a 'commoner' not royal. Her godmother was Mrs Arthur James (1861-1948) daughter of the Rt. Hon George Cavendish Bentinck, a wealthy woman with some American ancestry. Mrs James was an active member of the Wards Committee of Manor Gardens Centre and the American Women's Club of London. She undoubtedly encouraged the Duchess of York's interest in the Centre.

It is interesting to reflect on a certain mutuality of interest in royal patronage. We have become used to the notion of the British monarchy 're-inventing' itself both to keep up with the times, to get closer to the people, remain popular and survive social change. The leading authority of the history of philanthropy in Britain, Frank Prochaska, has coined the term 'welfare monarchy' to refer to this phenomenon, especially in the 1920s and 1930s (see Prochaska 1995).

The Duchess and the Duke of York had been frequent guests of honour at Lady Domini Crosfield's fundraising parties at *Witanhurst*, where the Wimbledon stars were introduced to them. The Duke himself played tennis there, sometimes watched by his young daughter Elizabeth. After the War this tradition was maintained by

The Duchess of York and Lady Crosfield in 1928.

Princess Elizabeth and Princess Margaret. The Duchess made a number of 'private' visits to the Centre. On 28 June 1928 she opened the new extension with the rather formulaic but nonetheless welcome words:

'I have very much pleasure in declaring this extension open and would like to wish you every success in your great and wonderful work.'

She named the main hall The Princess Elizabeth Hall after her two-year-old daughter. Domini Crosfield presented Florence Keen with a ceremonial silver trowel and in a short speech said of her that she was:

A mother and daughter wearing the father's medals at the visit of the Duchess of York in 1928.

'the mainspring of the whole movement of the Centre. From the outset she had thrown herself enthusiastically and unsparingly in to the work. No effort had been too great, no task too hard for her to tackle; and it seemed incredible that so much had been accomplished in 15 years, handicapped as they were by the four years of war.'

Mr Dooley, a member of the Fathers Committee, spoke of her as 'the Florence Nightingale of North Islington'.

When the Duke of York succeeded to the throne in 1936 as George VI, the Duchess became Queen Elizabeth, the Queen Consort. She kindly took the initiative in remaining our Patron. The following year she paid a formal visit to the Centre. The letter received from a Lady-in-Waiting at Buckingham Palace said:

'I must explain that the question of Patronages has been rather difficult to settle, as a good many have had to be dropped, as well as new ones adopted, but I am very happy to say that it is the special wish of The Queen to retain her connection with the North Islington Centre'.

SUCCESS STORY

In 1948 Queen Elizabeth paid us another formal visit. These events were of course carefully planned, with dress rehearsals and a red carpet borrowed from the Mayor. Following the death of her husband in 1952 she became Elizabeth the Queen Mother. At each of these stages she expressed her wish to renew her Patronage which was to continue until her death in 2002 aged 102. She visited us again in 1965, and for the last time on the occasion of our 75th anniversary in 1988, when she was 88.

On one occasion her Secretary had written to say that she would be unable to attend that year because she was too busy. Althea Davis, who by then could claim a certain degree of friendship and the privilege of a similarly advanced age, famously wrote back saying that this was ridiculous and that the Queen Mother must be able to fit us in. A reply duly came saying that the Queen's staff had indeed been able to manage to arrange this.

1923 was the first year in which the Duchess of York had undertaken to become President or Patron of charitable organisations. Those from that year that survived until her death in 2002 were:

Soldiers', Sailors' and Airmen's Forces Association
Victorian League for Commonwealth Friendship
The Royal Hospital for Nervous Disability
The Royal School of Needlework
The Royal Hospital for Sick Children, Glasgow
The Girls Brigade, Scotland
The Manor Gardens Welfare Trust

On her 100th birthday celebrations at Horse Guards Parade, the Centre was one of the more than three hundred organisations in the UK of which the Queen Mother was currently Patron, and who enjoyed her special inspiration and support. Our Director Frank Wood and a small team carried the Centre's banner in the very informal and friendly march past.

At her death in 2002 Elizabeth, Duchess of York, Queen Consort and Queen Mother, had been our Royal Patron for an astonishing 79 years.

PART THREE

Wartime

The First World War

'Wartime', that is the two World Wars and pre- and post-war conditions, occupied nearly half of the Centre's first forty years. There was little warning, let alone preparation, for the civilian population in 1914. By contrast detailed discussion of plans for wartime emergencies were to begin at least two years before the outbreak of war in 1939. The length of the aftermath of these major wars is hard to assess. In many ways conditions for the civilian population were worse during these periods. The post-war period after 1945 was not complete until about 1951 with the end of most rationing. A Londoner from the East End recalled her experience of visiting the Festival of Britain in summer 1951 as 'a release from the war'.

Within ten months of the Centre opening in late 1913, Britain was at war. The conflict was to affect the Centre's work incrementally. There were the casualties of the younger men, and later on of married men with families, the Zeppelin bombing raids, price increases and shortages, and the involvement of the Americans after 1917. On 29 September 1917 the Great Northern Hospital was hit by a bomb and there were non-fatal casualties. Work expanded. We never closed.

There was a strong feeling from the start that the Centre's work played a crucial role on 'the home front'. Newspapers were full of jingoism and sometimes unpleasantly eugenicist and racist statements about breeding a stronger race of British people. A diluted popular version of this was probably quite widespread. In any case the grim statistics of war underlined the value of the health and survival of the next generation. The annual report for 1917 refers to a talk by a visiting speaker, Dr Tchaykovsky, who made a comparison between numbers of soldiers killed and wounded and number of babies dying in infancy or rendered severely disabled in the year 1915:

Soldiers (1915 UK):	killed at the Front 75,000	wounded 500,000
Babies (1915 UK)	died in first year 1,000,000	physically unfit 1,500,000

WARTIME

Members of all social classes volunteered to fight. Working-class areas of Islington contributed disproportionately. Local anti-German feelings were exacerbated by the presence of some 3,000 German prisoners of war who were housed in the Cornwallis Road Workhouse. In 1917 the building was 'stormed' on four successive nights and had to be defended by Special Constables. Campbell Road (known as Campbell Bunk, 'the worst street in North London') just north of Seven Sisters Road near Holloway Road is said to have sent several hundred volunteers. Both areas were within the Centre's catchment area. A similar area even closer to home, also marked on Booth's socio-economic map of London at the lowest end of the scale, was that now occupied by Whittington Park: Milton Grove, Hampden Road, Cromwell Road and Rupert Street – a suitably imbalanced political choice of names. In the Park today is a memorial stone, once fixed to a building, listing 21 names of young men from one street alone, Cromwell Road, who died serving in the First World War. They include three pairs of brothers. The road may have had about 60 houses with a population of about 500 or more people. No ranks are given; almost certainly the majority were private soldiers. For many, in the short time before their death, it may well have been their first taste of regular employment and a good diet.

Six of these soldiers were with the Middlesex Regiment. Florence Keen's elder sons served in the 1/7 Middlesex Regiment: William Allen Keen (b. 1889) and Arthur Clive Keen (b. 1891). Both were Captains. Arthur was killed in action on 10 May 1917 and William died of wounds on 6 September 1918. Neither was married. They had both been subscribers to the Centre. This personal loss had a strong effect on Florence's personality. Her family suggest that she sought refuge and release from her grief and pain in her work for the Centre. We shall discuss this further later on.

In 1916 a new Military Service Act provided for the compulsory enlistment of married men of certain ages. The Centre began to receive letters from husbands at the front expressing their appreciation for the care offered by the Centre for their families. Florence Keen said in 1917 that 'The School [Centre] in so far as it was concerned with the wives and children of soldiers was definitely involved in war work'.

Among donations to the Centre at this time were several from war related sources: The Queen's War Relief Workshop; The Women of Australia (War Emergency Corps); The State of Queensland; The American Women's War Relief Fund (London).

Even before the entry of the USA into the war the American Women's Club Committee in London had begun to take an interest in the work of the Centre, as we have noted earlier. The combined contributions of the AWC, Mrs Leeds and the American Red Cross, backed by the American Embassy in London made a significant difference to our fortunes at a difficult time.

Military casualties on the Allied side were far greater in the First World War but the effect of bombing on the civilian home population was more intense in the Second World War. Zeppelin bombing raids on Islington in 1915 and 1917 caused damage and extreme alarm and anxiety, but casualties and infrastructural damage were slight compared with the bombing of cities and the London 'Blitz' in 1940-41 and the V1 and V2 pilot-less plane and rocket raids on London and the South East of England in 1944. The first bomb ever dropped on London from an aeroplane is recorded as having landed on Highbury Fields in 1917. Holloway Tube station was used as an air raid shelter in the First World War and later in the Second.

Both wars saw price increases and shortages of basic commodities, but only in World War II was a system of rationing of food, clothes and fuel developed.

Official records and even popular memories tend to exaggerate the spirit of optimism and courage. These and other virtues were abundantly present. But there was much more anxiety, fear and depression than is often allowed. The Centre in both wars played a tremendous part in consoling and counselling, as well as physically helping the bereaved and the fatherless. In 1917 Florence Keen speaks of the mothers of soldiers: 'Their need for the help and fellowship given at our School for Mothers has increased a hundredfold'.

During the First World War the North Library was used as a hospital for officers, an annexe of the Great Northern Hospital where 2,045 men were treated.

Islington's First World War memorial was a new Casualty Wing and Nurses' Hostel, paid for by public subscription and Islington's War Memorial Fund. This was demolished when the Hospital closed in 1992. It has been replaced by residential housing and a park, the Royal Northern Gardens. The Arch and Memorial Wall inscribing the names of Islingtonians who lost their lives in the war was opened in 1933 and remains in place in Manor Gardens. It is the focus of an annual Remembrance Sunday ceremony.

The Second World War

The Second World War had a more momentous impact on the Centre. Some of this was due to specific wartime conditions, such as requisitioning, evacuation, air raid protection, enlistment of staff, rationing and emergency nationalisation and 'pooling' of resources. At the same time the war hastened the development of the welfare state. Social and health measures begun in the 1930s were generalised. Plans for post-war social and economic changes were begun early on, notably in the Beveridge Plan of 1942. This foreshadowed the National Health Act which came into effect in 1948 after more than two years of detailed planning.

The Centre was obliged to work ever more closely with the local authorities, and overall this can be judged a success. On 22 June 1942 Dr Freeman, Islington's Medical Officer of Health, is recorded in the annual report as saying:

'The Borough Council has made use of the Centre premises since the beginning of the war and of the help of Miss Agnes Davies [the Superintendent Nurse] which was perhaps even more valuable. She had done an excellent job in the First Aid Posts, without any detriment to her duties at the Centre. The war had made the contact between the Centre and the Borough Council even closer and more beneficial to both'.

WARTIME

The earliest involvement of the Centre with wartime planning was in December 1937 when first discussions about air raid precautions took place. The following year all staff (including doctors, nurses, cooks and porters) attended Air Raid Protection (ARP) lectures and were issued with ARP badges. The next major concern from 1938 on was preparing for the evacuation of expectant mothers and mothers of children under five. Expectant mothers and babies would travel by train, others by coach. Women of the Women's Voluntary Service (WVS, later Royal Women's Voluntary Service) were trained at the Centre to be able to accompany evacuees, but they were not involved in accompanying unaccompanied children over the age of five. Centre staff had responsibilities for the registration of potential evacuees and the issue of gas masks and 'babies' helmets'.

Another wartime responsibility was the fair, orderly and regular distribution of food supplements, not only to registered Centre members but also to the general public. For example in 1942 the Centre distributed weekly: 1,000 bottles of orange juice, 150 bottles of cod liver oil and 250 packets of dried milk, as well as grocery parcels to 'necessitous mothers'. Centre staff also collected and sold clothing and organised 'make do and mend' classes.

The Compensation (Defence) Act of 1939 valued the Centre at a rental of £854 and the schedule of furniture at £142.17.6. 'Requisitioning' followed. Nos. 6 and 7 Manor Gardens were requisitioned to be lodgings for a 'Light Rescue Party' of paramedics and stretcher-bearers – the basement ceilings of Nos. 6 and 7 were reinforced with steel. This meant the closure of the Wards and fifteen staff were given notice. Most were reassigned to ARP and first aid duties: nurses (5), cook (1), maids (2), laundresses (3) and home helps (2). In addition two nurses were conscripted and posted to the front line in France. Meals were no longer offered by the Centre.

An air raid warning as early as 3 September 1939 'brought streams of anxious young parents to the Centre clamouring to be sent away. By superhuman effort arrangements were made for all those who wanted to go'. After a period of what has been called 'phoney war' 35% of evacuees returned. The flow was reversed during the heavy bombing raids from August 1940 to early 1941 and the rocket (V1 and V2) raids from June 1944 to March 1945.

Domini Crosfield, helped by Mrs Kingsley Curtis, had taken over Florence Keen's commanding role since just before the outbreak of war and continued with the same energy, leadership and optimism. In a minute dated 22 June 1942 she reflects that 'In spite of the difficulties created by the war, it was still possible to present the yearly report to the end of March 1942 on an optimistic note'. The report was shorter however, and lacked statistics, in order to save paper. Fundraising from two 'Flag Days' was better than ever: Princess Elizabeth Day (£121) and Alexandra Day (£195).

Harold Hugh Keen, the third and only surviving son of Florence, had been Treasurer since the late 1930s. He registered the strongest reaction to requisitioning, calling it 'commandeering' and 'catastrophic news', a 'grievous disruption'. The rebuilding plans were shelved and never revived. Hugh Keen volunteered for the RAF after his mother's death in 1942 and was promoted to Flight Lieutenant. He

Serious damage was inflicted on the Royal Northern Hospital on 9 September 1940.

survived and was 'demobbed' (demobilised) in 1945. He then resigned as Treasurer and went to Oxford University as 'Keeper of the University Chest' and Fellow of Balliol College.

In 1940-41 37,296 homes in Islington were destroyed or damaged, most beyond easy repair. Islington suffered another blow in 1944 when Hitler launched the V1 and V2 raids on South-East England. From February 1944 onwards requests for evacuation began again. These were random, unpredictable raids intended to cause terror. Eighteen of these bombs or rockets fell on Islington, though most fell short of London or were destroyed in the air. The General Post Office building in Manor Gardens had 'roof spotters' to warn of the impending fall of the silent rockets. In June 1944 Domini Crosfield requested that the warning of 'overhead danger' should be extended to the Centre. Mothers and children were required to lie on the floor in case of attack and stay away from windows. Upper windows were covered with wire netting against the danger of flying glass. But the mothers did not stop attending. During the course of the war the Centre had some near misses. A bomb fell on a corner of the Royal Northern Hospital on 9 September 1940, just two hundred yards from the Centre. It destroyed two eight-bed wards and two labour wards. Following normal procedure the mothers and babies had been moved for the night to a secure area. There were no serious injuries. The Hospital moved to a prepared site near Welwyn Garden City. Another bomb damaged the Centre's printer's workshop. The most serious nearby destruction was close to the Odeon on the Holloway Road (where the present Post Office is) and in Eden Grove near the railway line by Holloway Road tube station. Pentonville prison received a bomb attack. 26 people died at Highbury Corner on 27 June 1944 killed by a V1 attack that also demolished the fine building above Highbury Station and part of Compton Terrace. More serious damage was done in the south of the borough and Finsbury. Sadly the worst fatalities were in buildings where people had gathered for safety: Northampton College (now City University) where 400 lost their lives and Dame Alice Owen's School (over 100). The curious paid one penny to see bomb craters and damage, in aid of 'the Spitfire Fund'.

Apart from this murderous period, 1944 saw gradually improving conditions. Nurses were released from air raid emergency duties. On 26

Invitation to the AGM in 1945.

THE CHAIRMAN AND COMMITTEE
OF THE
NORTH ISLINGTON INFANT WELFARE CENTRE
REQUEST THE PLEASURE OF YOUR COMPANY AT THEIR

ANNUAL GENERAL MEETING

ON MONDAY, JUNE 11th, 1945, at 3.30 p.m.
IN THE
PRINCESS ELIZABETH HALL, MANOR GARDENS, N.7.

Speakers : HIS WORSHIP THE MAYOR OF ISLINGTON
DR. HADEN GUEST, M.C., M.P.
DR. K. M. HIRST, Acting M.O.H., Islington.

TEA 4.30 p.m.

R.S.V.P., Hon. Sec.,
8/9, Manor Gardens, N.7.

Princess Elizabeth with Lady Crosfield at Witanhurst in 1951.

January 1944 the requisitioning of Nos. 6 and 7 and the central building came to an end. It was not until November 1945 however that the Civil Defence Services checked on needs for structural alterations to the Centre following de-requisitioning. The cost was determined at £1,360. In 1944 correspondence with the King's Fund was reopened with regard to restarting the wards. By the end of 1944 the tide of war had turned, even if 'the struggle for Europe' was far from over. Further bombing of London was not foreseen The Centre recovered its property and began to rebuild its resources.

Domini Crosfield, Mrs Kingsley Curtis and the Chief Superintendent Nurse Miss Davies and a number of other staff and volunteers had continued to serve the Centre throughout the war. These included Dr Campbell, now Lady Maxwell, whose husband was the Head of the Home Office throughout the war. They had fulfilled their intention stated at the outset that the Centre would sustain as far as possible the promotion of the health of children and the education of mothers. And this in spite of 'the shadow of fear and uncertainty'. In fact in 1944 there were more babies registered than there had been in 1939.

Even before the end of the war there was talk of 'municipalisation' and 'nationalisation', some form of radical restructuring of health services. The outcomes of this will be dealt with in the next chapters. One feature of working more closely with local and central government, intensified by war time circumstances, was pervasive petty bureaucratisation: filling forms, seeking permissions and reporting in detail. While some of this was inevitable and necessary, much was an excessive burden on the time and patience of staff. More importantly it sapped some of the friendly, local, independent and maybe idiosyncratic atmosphere that made up the spirit of the Centre.

The War in Europe ended on 7 May 1945, that with Japan on 14 August the same year. On 11 June 1945 the Centre held its first General Meeting following the cessation of hostilities. It was an open meeting. We were ready for a very different and even more challenging time ahead.

Domini Crosfield resumed her fundraising tennis parties in 1946. Her invitation lists 73 'Patrons' of the event. It is an interesting post-war line-up. The patrons, or senior contributing guests included the ambassadors of five Allied European countries: and three others. Amongst various other aristocrats, generals and celebrities were:

Mrs C[lement].R. Attlee
Mrs Winston Churchill
Lady Megan Lloyd-George
Mr and Mrs J.B. Priestley
Noel Coward
The Rt. Hon. Philip Noel-Baker MP
The Hon. Mrs Arthur Burns
Mrs Helena Venizelou
The Lord Chancellor (Viscount Jowett)
Viscount Rothermere (Cecil Harmsworth)
Viscount Templewood (Sir Samuel Hoare).

PART FOUR

Reflections on Leadership

Florence Keen, a biographical reflection

In broad terms Florence Keen's adult life may be divided into two phases: before and after she started the Centre in 1913. She married William Brock Keen (aged 28) in 1887 at the age of 19. Her five children were born in 1889, 1891, 1894 (twins) and 1902 respectively. Her husband had set up a prospering firm of accountants in the City of London. He was already well-to-do and soon became very wealthy from his professional work. He had the cachet of having come first in the very first examination held by the Institute of Chartered Accountants. By about 1890 he had bought *Mayfield* on West Hill, Highgate, while maintaining a large shared family house called *Edgehill* at Limpsfield, in Surrey. Florence settled into Highgate making many friends, and the Keen family became leading lights in its high society. Their fine house with its tennis courts hosted many musical and sporting parties. Her children, both boys and girls went to the best private schools.

Like her friend Domini Crosfield, Florence was an excellent pianist, as were her children. She also enjoyed the relaxing occupation of gardening especially at *Edgehill*. This combination of calm and frenetic activity is beautifully captured in a water-colour painting by her daughter-in-law Catherine in about 1935, reproduced in this volume. The scene is a tranquil and privileged drawing room at *Mayfield*. Hugh Keen (the painter's husband) is playing a grand piano. W.B. Keen is sitting listening, wearing a three-piece tweed suit with plus four trousers. A maid is coming through the door with a tray carrying two glasses and what is probably a decanter of whisky and a soda syphon. Florence's corner of the room occupies nearly half the space. She is wearing a long skirt with her legs very wide apart in a determined and assertive pose. It is hard to read her features but they seem to be a mixture of quite placid and fairly grim, not relaxed. But what sets the tone are the objects surrounding her. A small table bears her medicines. On the floor is a little lap desk with ink, pens and stationery. An attaché case is overflowing with papers. Several other papers and two books lie carelessly about the floor at her feet, and the large waste paper basket is full. She is holding a scroll of some sort. There is a small knitted infant's garment on the floor and a ball of wool with knitting needles through it.

It is interesting to note that while both Florence and her husband had backgrounds that were by and large liberal and non-conformist, she was rather

Florence Keen, her husband and surviving son Hugh at Mayfield, Highgate, in about 1935. It was painted by Hugh's wife Catherine. (Courtesy of their son Charles Keen.)

more radically inclined. Apart from the evidence of her later work, we have noted that two of her long-standing friends in 1913 who became leading activists in the Centre, Ada Wallas and Nora Hobhouse, were married to a socialist and a radical liberal respectively. Mrs Keen's circle of friends included numerous people with titles of nobility and aristocracy, though these were more likely to be people who, or whose recent ancestors, were ennobled for services to the professions, industry and commerce, as much as to politics or the military etc. We have already established the importance of this cohort of supporters for the Centre.

Florence was 46 in 1913 and she remained active on behalf of the Centre until her death aged 74 in 1942. This second phase might be sub-divided as follows:

1913-14 the Centre pre-war
1915-19 the Centre as 'war work'
1920-30 the Centre as Florence's 'anodyne', after the death of her sons
1930-38 period of crises, retirement
1939-42 period of reduced activity on the sidelines

Angel to Mothers

A WOMAN
HUNDREDS
BLESS

She Saved Their
Babies' Lives

By a Special Correspondent

BEHIND the announcement of a broadcast appeal to-morrow is the romance of the woman whom mothers call the real " Angel of Islington."

Mr. Howard Marshall is to talk of the work of the North Islington Infant Welfare Centre and School for Mothers, which was founded in 1913 by Mrs. A. M. Keen, its present secretary, a gracious silver-haired woman.

" She is the real angel of Islington," one of the mothers told me. " She saved my baby's life.

" She has saved hundreds of us mothers and babies in Islington. God bless her."

NINE IN A ROOM

There are 2,000 mothers who come regularly to the centre, some of them indescribably poor.

" I have found 11 people living in two rooms, with no water and no gas,' said Mrs. Keen. " One of our mothers lives with her husband and seven children in one room. Families in this neighbourhood average seven children. In 1913 many families had between 15 and 17 children.

" The depression has hit our people very hard. They have nothing left to pawn and they can't borrow any more.

" Four years ago we had no rickets ; in the past year we have had 214 cases."

GRATEFUL FATHERS

The centre is a place of jollity and activity all day long. There are ten clinics for children, four for mothers, two dental and six sunlight clinics every week.

The enthusiasm and devotion are remarkable. The fathers raised £57 for the Centre by organising dances last year. One " difficult " mother who could say nothing but " I can't " or " I won't," now spends all her time persuading other mothers to come to the centre.

An appreciation of Florence Keen, from the News Chronicle 31 March, 1934

It is important to note that this characterisation refers to her personal involvement and motivation, not those of the Centre as a whole. In what follows I make particular use of oral and some written evidence from members of her family.

In 1913 'neither she nor anyone guessed at the time the famous future that awaited this undertaking or the endless consequences it was to have for her and her family'. She made it clear that she wanted to make infant welfare her 'war work'. Then in 1917 and 1918 her two older sons were killed in action. She suffered most terribly from this loss. 'Post-traumatic stress disorder' was not then a notion in use. Even the term 'shell shock' as a precursor to modern diagnosis was still debatable. Her youngest son wrote:

'Superficially my mother was very brave. She carried on with all her normal activities and did not give way or collapse. But her horrors were simply thrust below the surface, never confronted or assimilated, never come to terms with. She could neither understand

nor forgive Fate for the blow it had dealt her and her sense of outrage more than grief itself ... progressively corroded her spirit ... By way of anodyne she drove herself frenziedly at her infant welfare work'.

Florence probably gave proportionately less attention to her twin daughters Ursula and Barbara, and perhaps her surviving son, Hugh. Dr Jessie Campbell (née Maxwell), an old family friend, is said to have been 'like a mother' to the girls.

Things never improved; they became progressively worse. 'She was soon worn to a ravelling both physically and nervously and so remained for the rest of her life'. Her son recalled that only occasionally were there 'hours and days and periods when she was like her old self, lively, festive, charming'. In the 1930s there were nation-wide epidemics of infant gastro-enteritis. Two babies died in the Manor Gardens Centre Wards. As part of a normal routine the Ministry of Health sent an Inspector, a young and inexperienced woman doctor. She wrote a sharply critical report. It seems that it was intended to emphasise what more could be done rather than allocate blame for past practice. In any case Florence took it hard and fought to have it withdrawn. In the end the report was modified and she received a personal letter praising her previous work and the Centre's high reputation. Nonetheless 'It was a savage blow at my mother's life's work and wounded her to the quick and made her mad with rage'. In the years that followed she was anxious about creeping municipalisation, which she 'took as a personal insult'.

Florence Keen's health declined and she resigned in 1938. She was awarded the OBE in 1937. She retired to her house, *Edgehill*, in Limpsfield, Surrey but kept up a steady correspondence with Domini Crosfield. She sometimes offered advice and comments, but always in a most polite and restrained manner. She devoted her attention increasingly to her husband. The staff and mothers put up a memorial to him after his death which read:

William Brock Keen
a faithful and unsparing
friend of the Centre
from its foundation
until his death in 1941

this tablet was placed here by the staff
and mothers in grateful remembrance

Not long before his death, his offices at 23 Queen Victoria Street, London EC4 were bombed on Sunday morning 11 May 1941.

Florence had worked closely with devoted colleagues, the doctors – several of whom were close personal friends – the Chief Superintendent and others. She had the respectful, even adoring, support of many hundreds, thousands of mothers, fathers and volunteers. Her style was hands-on and leading by example. She was a

Destruction of William Keen's business premises in Queen Victoria Street during the London blitz of 1941.

dominant and many would say domineering figure. Her son wrote 'She was a great one for telling people what to do'. Nonetheless she was a teacher and enabler and encouraged the participation of parents. She spent long hours at the Centre and took work home with her, using the billiard room as an office. Her husband is reported as having said that 'Of course at the Centre she is the Empress'. A last quotation from Hugh Keen's perceptive memoir sums up much of her style of work:

'She did indeed believe passionately in voluntary service, set the highest possible standards in her work and had that personal magnetism that could make people perform in a way they would not have thought themselves capable of. And she, very rightly, believed in an absence of rules so that when she saw a need she could instantly fill it by some form of improvisation'.

It was a sad irony that when Florence retired to live at *Edgehill* during the Second World War her house, 'paradise' as one member of the family recalls, was hit by an enemy bomb. Florence and her husband were having breakfast in the dining room of this extensive building when a High Explosive bomb fell on the further end. They recounted seeing furniture flying through the air but they were unharmed, and it seems, unruffled. A friend telephoned to say she must come and visit them, to which Florence replied, with her usual sangfroid: 'that would not be convenient, my dear, as we have an unexploded land mine in the garden'.

Bureaucratisation and charismatic leadership

The Manor Gardens Centre exists in a social space known as 'civil society', between so to say private and local life and the structures of government. Other terms that overlap with this are the charitable, voluntary or 'third' sector. Why does it matter that such organisations as Manor Gardens continue to flourish? Some key background assumptions are:

1 That while a 'national' health service and national welfare services and statutory provisions are essential for the well being of the people of the UK, such services will never exhaust or fully provide for all the particular and local health and welfare needs of a rapidly changing society.

2 That voluntary service has a social and moral value in itself.

3 That 'civil society' represents a resource of immense importance, able to develop alternative practices, and to propose and campaign for reforms independently from political parties and state structures.

In its dealings with government this third sector has to be absolutely up to the mark in the regulation and accountability of its own practices. And it has to be keenly aware of the need to avoid being used or exploited by government to take on tasks that should properly be undertaken by statutory authorities or that risk dilution of the voluntary ethos.

Sociologists have concepts that are useful for our discussion. One is 'bureaucratisation' which refers to the process of standardisation, routinisation and regulation that can make an institution efficient and sustainable. At one extreme, in its pejorative sense, it refers to an overregulated and self-serving organisation.

Another term 'charismatic leadership' refers to a type of leadership and its following. Charisma is originally a theological term meaning a divinely conferred power or talent and is more broadly used to denote a capacity to inspire devotion and enthusiasm. In the sociological model charismatic forms of organisation are inherently unstable and may die out when their initial impetus or leader passes on, or they may become 'routinised' and 'bureaucratised'. The history of the Manor Gardens Centre provides a good instance of 'charismatic leadership' and its transformations.

The notion of charismatic leadership focuses on the style of leadership. Typically this is an individual with exceptional motivation, intelligence, physical energy and presence, and personal charm. These qualities are combined with a strictness of moral discipline and self-sacrifice. One of the key elements is a sort of personal 'magnetism', aura or powers of attraction that we find in the popular use of the term 'charismatic', whether to refer to footballers or religious sectarians.

The charismatic leader relies on a personal following with a core of dedicated friends and lieutenants, and a wider set of dedicated followers and volunteers drawn in by a feeling of admiration bordering on adoration.

The mission and style of work are original and innovative. Spontaneity and improvisation predominate over regulation and systematisation. There is strong reliance on voluntary, unpaid recruits.

The organisation is funded by donations rather than any standard levies or taxes.

Succession is problematic. Often there are short dynastic lines whether familial or 'apostolic'. There is a tendency towards reverence for a deceased founder, or for ancestor worship.

As we celebrate our hundredth anniversary in 2013 we know that the Centre has indeed been sustained. More than that, it is viable and full of promise for the future. This suggests that the Centre may be a good case study for comparative research as it manifests the progression from a form of charismatic leadership to a more sustainable, rational form of management and governance that avoids the extremes of bureaucratisation.

The Manor Gardens Centre's distinctive history shows that it had to operate on two fronts. It was fiercely independent and yet it needed good will and funding from government authorities. It was well regulated internally to the extent it found necessary. It relied more on volunteers than paid staff. Its own records and accounts were most meticulously prepared. This must owe a lot to Mr W.B. Keen who was a statistician as well as an accountant. In a new 'modern' post-war spirit it tried to be open, participatory and to a degree 'democratic'. This may be shown in the numerous committees that were set up, though it must be recalled that Florence Keen was active and influential on all of them, except the Fathers Committee. To some extent Keen's influence was shared by other leading figures, notably Domini Crosfield and the leading lights of the American Women's Wards Committee. This ensured continuity after Keen's death. The Keen family involvement was to continue into the fourth generation until the retirement of her grandson Tim Davis in 2002, and resignation of his son-in-law Robert Warner in 2007.

With the appointment in 1979 of a full-time senior administrator (or Director and then Chief Executive Officer), with increasing scrutiny by the Charity Commissioners and the coming of the so-called 'contract culture' from the 1990s, the Centre has become ever more regulated and indeed well managed. Although all the core work is now done by paid staff, our list of volunteer project workers has never been longer. The Board of Trustees, which is entirely voluntary and unremunerated, is more active than ever. We shall return to these considerations at the end of our story.

PART FIVE

NHS and after –
a kind of independence

Municipalisation and Nationalisation

We have seen that the Centre has worked in partnership with government health authorities from the earliest days, at the level of the Borough of Islington, the London County Council (LCC and then GLC) and the Ministry of Health, after it had been set up in 1919. The Islington Borough Medical Officer of Health sat on our General Committee from its first meetings. The names of Dr A.E. Harrison (MOH 1913-1921), Dr Clark Trotter (MOH 1921-41) and Dr Victor Freeman (MOH 1941-64) are prominent in our records. They were good supporters of the Centre. This link was broken in 1948.

By the beginning of the Second World War the proportion of the Centre's income coming from the public sector exceeded the voluntary component. It continued to increase as a proportion. The Centre may have been apprehensive about creeping municipalisation in the 1930s but it had to be admitted that the nation's health care provision was inadequate for the task, was a mixed bag of organisations of varying quality and efficiency, and was especially lacking in equitable distribution of benefits. Wartime conditions focused the minds of the planners even more intensely and as early as 1942 the Beveridge Plan foreshadowed a radical new post-war settlement and patterns of health and welfare services.

The 30th Annual Report for 1943/44 contains a thoughtful piece which is worth citing at some length.

'Among the most important and difficult questions to answer when considering a national health service is the question of the existence of voluntary bodies within the structure. What would be their functions and position? ...

When one considers ... the pioneer work carried out by the North Islington Infant Welfare Centre, and reflects that it is typical of many similar efforts, one may perhaps hope that eventually the relationship between public and voluntary enterprises may be so adjusted as to relieve voluntary bodies of the burden of constant struggle to raise funds for maintenance, while safeguarding their freedom of experiment and elasticity of method.

Pioneer work, research and experiment are vital to social progress, and all experience shows that freedom and audacity are more frequently found in voluntary than in public enterprise, largely because a voluntary committee can raise private funds and run financial risks to put into practice schemes as yet unsupported by public opinion, in a way impossible for a body responsible exclusively for public funds.

The National Health Service should, therefore, be a partnership, on terms so drawn up as to allow each partner to give his best in the service of all.'

It was to take nearly three years of hard work and negotiation between the election of the Labour Government in 1945 and the coming into force of the NHS Act on 5 July 1948. The Act itself had been passed in 1946. In the meantime and in anticipation, there was a distinct process of further municipalisation. The chief issue for the Centre – and the three other Islington voluntary infant welfare centres – was management of Health Visitors (HVs). Inevitably there were demands for greater uniformity and regulation in matters of duties, hours, dress and procedures.

Domini Crosfield and Mrs Kingsley Curtis went to the Ministry of Health to discuss this. The Conjoint Committee discussed it, and on 18 December 1944 it agreed to accept the principle of municipalisation of HVs on certain conditions, which seem to have been accepted:

1 HVs to be appointed by a selection committee comprising half local authority and half Centre members.

2 HVs to be appointed proportionately to the distribution of the child population.

3 HVs to operate from the Centres.

4 HVs' caseload should include six half days visiting and three half days supervising clinics.

In 1944/5 the number of HVs (for children under five) in Islington was as follows:

employer	number of children	number of HVs	caseload per HV
Borough	8,000	8	1,000
Centres	6,000	15	400

This shows that the level of care provided by the Centre HVs was likely to be greater, and that they were able to treat Centre members more holistically; and also that they had more rounded and rewarding jobs.

Negotiations with the Ministry of Health and Aneurin Bevan

The leading figures in the Centre kept up pressure on the MoH in the years prior to the implementation of the NHS Act. They made numerous visits to senior officers

Aneurin Bevan MP, 1897-1965.

in several departments. This culminated in a famous meeting with the Minster of Health Aneurin Bevan (1897-1965, Minister of Health August 1945 - January 1951). There is no doubt that this meeting took place but there are no records that we have been able to trace. The few details are from oral traditions and much later interviews. The Centre fielded its 'A Team':

Lady Crosfield, whose friends now included Violet Attlee, wife of the Prime Minister;

Lady Maxwell, whose husband had been Perm-anent Secretary at the Home Office throughout the war and after. She had been one of the pioneer doctors at the centre;

Althea Davis, daughter of Florence Keen and now Hon. Secretary.

It can only be presumed that the MoH saw sufficient good, rational reasons for permitting the continuing independence of the Centre and that they were persuaded by the Centre's advocates. The assumption at the time was that incorporation into the NHS would take place unless there were compelling reasons to exempt. It is not hard to imagine that there might have been some personal factors at work. One person interviewed has suggested that somehow the Centre's forceful and brilliant team overawed Bevan, and even that he may have given up in exasperation. Such is the stuff of legend. Jeremy Corbyn, Labour MP for Islington North since 1983, has offered another idea for at least a contributory factor. This is that the Centre had an affinity and positive association in Bevan's mind with the coal miners' welfare groups in Ebbw Vale in South Wales where he was brought up.

As if to underline our continuity of independence on 9 June 1948 Queen Elizabeth our Royal Patron, and her younger daughter Princess Margaret attended Lady

Crosfield's Garden Party in aid of the Centre.

On 5 July 1948 responsibility for maternal and child welfare services passed from the Borough of Islington to the London County Council (LCC) under the NHS. Islington was joined with Finsbury and Holborn to form one of nine London health and welfare regions.

The first three years of the Centre's experience of working alongside the LCC with respect to Health Visitors (1945-47) has been reported as having provided 'undoubted gain in cohesion and comprehensiveness of work'. The dangers of losing the essence of our voluntary work and ability to offer 'a more intimate and personal approach' seem to have been avoided or overcome.

The 1953/54 Annual Report reflects on six years of working with the NHS. The co-operation was described as 'harmonious'. The Centre's bargaining had ensured that half of funds raised on its own account could be used at the discretion of the Centre, the other half for maintenance. Later this was extended to all such funds.

The chief and very great benefit was relief from anxiety for provision of funding for basic services. The new national perspective of health provision also encouraged a wider view of the health needs of the community. 'But the falling off of the Welfare Fund [a discretionary fund to allow the poorest members to receive services at no cost to them] threatened the continuity of the Play Centre and the Holiday Scheme.'

This review in 1954 once again emphasised the distinctive contribution that the Centre could make through its voluntary ethos: '...there must be room for imagination, homeliness, and commonsense in dealing with problems so individual, and so unpredictable they cannot be wholly contained in an Act of Parliament'.

In 1960/61 Althea Davis reflects again on the relationship with the LCC within the NHS Act.

'We have always been very appreciative of the advantages and privileges of working with the huge structure of the National Health Service Act and we have grown up an increasingly co-operative understanding and cordiality between us and our local authority which is the LCC.' However there was some perception that voluntary service in the health sector was being down-valued which was a 'disparagement of the voluntary sector'.

The long anticipated and feared dependence under the NHS Act of 1948 had not materialised. The key elements of our independence had not been destroyed. The new relationship had been a success. This did not prevent the resignation of a few members of the Committee in 1950 who felt they could not work under the new dispensation. This did not cause any breach in the solidarity of the Committee.

The transfer of responsibility for health back to the Borough Council in 1963 was met with relief and renewed hope. Althea Davis reflected wisely and wittily in the following terms after the first year of this change. She shows awareness of the need continually to review and renew such partnerships.

NHS AND AFTER – A KIND OF INDEPENDENCE

'The first year, harnessed to new partners, is always a rather a testing time; more so perhaps for them rather than us. For us they have at least a recognisable shape whereas we may appear to them as something rather strange, rather large, rather elderly and sometimes thought to be a little cumbersome; rather like an elephant (possibly even a white elephant?).

This strangeness is partly due to our voluntary status which is a bit of a rarity nowadays. I think, too, that our title is a little cumbersome and misleading. If we dropped 'Infant' (very carefully!) and were known as the North Islington Welfare Centre it would be simpler and would indicate our recognition, which I am sure is shared by the Borough Council, that there are a good many activities which are not represented here, which should be, and which we are able and willing to develop. Let us not be impeded by unnecessary barriers or prejudices on either side from playing our full part in the widening field of preventative care.

We on our side have to be sure the new Authority is not going to over-run us or crowd us out or squash us flat. They on their side have to be sure we are not arrogant, pig-headed, rebellious and an out-dated nuisance.'

Changing of the guard

The 1940s saw a changing of the guard at the Centre. Of the two 'founding' doctors Dr Vance Ingram (née Knox) had left to live in Scotland in 1941. Florence Keen had died in 1942 and the following year Dr Jessie Maxwell (née Campbell), 'Cam', perhaps Florence's best friend, now Lady Maxwell, resigned from her medical post. She

Dr Jessie Maxwell.

Lady Domini Crosfield (1890-1962), who retired as Chairman in 1959. She had given 45 years of service to Manor Gardens.

continued to serve on the Committee and played a strategic role until her death in 1953. She had given 39 years of service to the Centre.

In 1946 Hugh Keen, Florence's youngest, and only surviving, son resigned as Treasurer after some years of war service. In the same year James Benjamin Reeves died. He had worked for W.B. Keen since the 1880s becoming senior partner. He had rendered the Centre much service as Hon. Auditor and as a generous donor. Also in 1946 Mrs Whitehouse died. She had been a Health Visitor since 1919. In 1949 two stalwart figures died: Miss Agnes Davies Nursing Superintendent and very much Florence Keen's 'Number Two'. We also lost Mrs Cracknell, the cook and general housekeeper.

By the 1950s the pioneers had passed on, including notably Mrs Edwards who joined the Committee in 1916, and served as Vice-Chairman 1936-54. A final sense of closure came with the retirement of Domini Crosfield as Chairman in 1959 and her death in 1963. She held her last tennis party in 1960. She had given the Centre some 45 years of service. She was presented with a retirement volume full of memories of her works. It was inscribed to 'Lady Crosfield, Chairman, North Islington Welfare Centre, 1919-1959, from her Colleagues, the Staff and the Mothers' Council'. Among the signatures were those of: Alexander Maxwell, Dr Eve Atkins and Mrs Cynthia Landeryou. After her death her papers were dispersed. Several letters appeared for sale on the Internet, some of which have been acquired by the Centre. The retirement volume was bought by the Islington Local History Centre where it is available for all to see.

New recruits and volunteers appeared to fill the gaps. Some had been in place since the war years.

Dr Eve Atkins

Eve Atkins had taken on the mantle of the pioneer doctors in 1942, at a difficult time. She remained active until her sadly early death aged 52 in 1963. She was a popular and talented doctor. She had qualified in 1935 and worked in the Elizabeth Garrett Anderson Hospital among others. She served as an anaesthetist at the Royal Northern Hospital helping with casualties of air raids during the war. She was becoming a prominent public figure, a founding members of the Royal College of General Practitioners and Council Member of the Medical Women's Federation. She was School Doctor at Channing School for Girls in Highgate, which was in turn a long-standing supporter of the Centre. She won several golfing prizes at Highgate Golf Club and was a keen skier and mountain walker. She enjoyed the rare privilege for a woman at that time of being elected a member of the United Services Flying Club. after she had learned to fly solo during the war.

Alan Fabes ACA

Alan Fabes had joined as Hon. Accountant in 1940. In this role and later as Hon. Treasurer, he played a vital role until 1977, subsequently joining the Executive Committee and then the Board of Trustees until 1997, an extraordinary 55 years of

Dr Eve Atkins., c. 1960, Doctor at the Centre 1942-63.

contribution. His mother had been a volunteer at the Centre in the 1930s.

In 1944 the Centre appointed for the first time a full-time administrator, or office manager, not quite a Director in the later sense, but a great relief to the long-serving Superintendent Nurse Agnes Davies.

Following Mrs Kingsley Curtis who had helped to oversee a period of 'interregnum' so to say, after Florence Keen's death, the latter's daughter Althea Davis (née Keen, often referred to as Mrs Edgar Davis) took the helm as Chairman and bridged the period from 1947 until 1977.

Althea Davis MBE 1894-1990

Althea was like her mother physically, tall, redheaded, and it seems resembled her somewhat in temperament, though having a greater sense of humour. She had some conflicts with her mother over her decision to convert from agnosticism to Roman Catholicism. She had been influenced by her friend Hildegaard von Hügel while doing charitable work in London. In consequence of her difficulties with Florence, Althea did not feel able to work alongside her. However, at the age of 54, several years after her mother's death, she felt free and committed enough to take on the demanding job of Hon. Secretary, the chief mover of the whole undertaking. After her retirement in 1975 she became President until shortly before her death in 1990 at the age of 96.

Althea's early education was with a governess at home. She was brought up with a Victorian strictness, seeing her parents only after tea. She then had an excellent schooling at Roedean School for Girls. She went on to Newnham College at Cambridge University, where she studied English and won sporting 'Blues' for representing Cambridge at tennis and cricket. Her writing style is memorialised in her many annual reports. After university, in the 1930s she worked in London with Hildegaard at the Queensbury Club for working girls and bought a house as a weekend retreat for them.

She went with Hildegaard to Berlin and became a fluent German speaker like

Althea Davis MBE, 1894-1962.

her brother Hugh. She also visited Austria and Czechoslovakia and began to help with the expatriation of Catholic Jews. At one point, her son Tim Davis recalled, she had some 80 of these refugees, predominantly children, in a house she bought for them, together with five nuns and a priest. This work was greatly assisted by Dr 'Cam' Maxwell and her husband Sir Alexander Maxwell the Permanent Secretary of State at the Home Office who had a pro-actively tolerant policy of helping the immigration of Jewish families from German occupied Europe and whenever possible releasing them from internment camps in Britain.

Ursula Carter (née Keen), Althea's daughter, made a significant contribution to the Centre but chose not to remain long. She did however train at the Centre to become a nursery nurse.

Some of the Centre's later activities may have clashed with Althea's catholic beliefs, but this seems never to have prevented any activity taking place. The clearest sign of this was that the Centre became host to a Roman Catholic Family Advisory Service, which catered for a much wider area than Islington, after the Centre had set up a Family Planning Clinic. Her antipathy, and that of her son, to openly homosexual lifestyles did not prevent The centre acting as host landlord to the

London Teenage Gay Organisation in the 1980s, whose activities we also managed. The Centre has always welcomed people and organisations of all faiths and none.

Althea clearly enjoyed working with Domini Crosfield. We have a handwritten letter from her to Paul, Domini's adopted son. She refers to some documents she is returning a year or two after his mother's death. The letter reads, in part:

'...what doesn't grow dim in my mind is what fun we had in those days. I suppose because although we were serious we were never solemn. And because your Mother, although sometimes alarming, was always such fun to work with. We who knew her remember her still with gratitude and delight'.

The rise and decline of mothers and babies clinics

The period after the implementation of the NHS Act was mostly 'business as usual' at the Centre. The main feature of this was the daily clinics for mothers and their babies. The following figures indicate the trends:

Year	women attending pre-natal clinics	all children attending aged 0-5 all clinics
1945	4,759	15,750
1950	na	22,184
1963	4,978	18,502
1973	299	7,607
1976	92	4,556
1978	8	3,352

The 1969 annual report expressed renewed concern about falling numbers. On the other hand that year showed the highest ever numbers, before or since, of children attending the Play Centre, 19,000 attendances. There are several obvious reasons for this decline in demand on the Centre, if not the need in the community. One was that the general level and advance in education of parents. Another was that GPs and local hospitals provided more of the services themselves.

The sunlight treatment ended in 1967 after some 45 years. The clinics continued to offer ante-natal and post-natal advice, day observation clinics, infant and mother massage, exercise classes, distribution of basic medicaments, vitamins etc., parenting advice, dietary advice, sewing and cooking classes. On top of this was the communal socialising among parents. Some of these services were to be continued after the closure of the baby clinics or were offered in different formats. But as we shall see the period after 1977 onwards is a distinctly different phase in the Centre's history. As it had long done, the Centre continued to provide additional services, sometimes at short notice and in response to particular and urgent needs. These included blood transfusion, polio, diphtheria and whooping cough immunisation, and cervical smear tests after 1972.

An early example of a new departure was the response of the Centre to needs of handicapped children (to use the term current at the time) and young adults. This was to remain an important strand in the work for many years.

Another issue, noted as early as 1952 was the mental health and wellbeing needs in the community. A specialist concern with mental wellbeing had been part of the Centre's practice from the start. Staff were well aware of the stresses and mental strains on mothers, whether pre-natal or post-natal, or from coping with a family life of poverty and deprivation. In times of war bereavement counselling for women became a specific task for the Health Visitors.

As life expectancy rose, and especially from 1972, the Centre increasingly turned its attention to the needs of some elderly people. We shall return to this and other themes raised in this section.

Immigration and a multi-ethnic society

Over many years the Centre has had an exemplary record of fairness as to equal opportunities, inclusiveness, social tolerance and lack of discrimination, often long before these values were enshrined in Acts of Parliament. Indeed the Centre set an example. Staff, clientele and volunteers have been a fair mixture of varieties of ethnic background. Before the large scale immigrations of the second half of the century, surnames suggest people from earlier migrations, Huguenot, Irish and Italian. The Irish born population had moved to Islington from Camden and Kilburn, the main points of entry. In 1984 one sixth (16.6%) of the population of North Islington had been born in Ireland and many more had Irish ancestry. Visitors from Africa and Asia tended to be from élite and professional strata of society.

The World Wars had brought to Britain numbers of Commonwealth citizens, including Caribbeans, of many different island cultures, either as members of the armed forces or to work in industry. But it was not until 1948 that there was a significant and increasing number of new arrivals and families. In that year the Labour Government passed the British Nationality Act that gave full British citizenship to all Commonwealth citizens. And in that same year, on 22 June 1948 the passenger ship *Empire Windrush* docked in Tilbury, London, with 493 passengers from the West Indies. Many found employment in the new National Health Service, and benefited from its services.

No restrictions were placed on the number of immigrants until 1962. The number of Caribbean born British citizens in 1950 had been 15,000. By 1961 this figure had risen to 132,000. By this time Caribbean mothers, babies and fathers had become frequent visitors to the Centre. In the 2001 national census 575,876 people identified themselves as 'Black Caribbean'.

During the 1950s there had been a slow and smaller immigration of Commonwealth citizens from Cyprus. This reached a peak of 25,000 in one year, 1960. Many settled in Haringey and neighbouring Northern Islington. By 1981 there were 160,000 British Cypriots. In the early years the proportions of Greek and Turkish speaking Cypriots coming to Britain were not far from their proportionate size in the population of Cyprus itself which has considerably more Greek speakers. By 2001, due to events in de-colonised Cyprus, the Turkish speaking population exceeded Greek speakers.

By 1961 approximately one-third of all visitors to the Centre were from the West Indies, Africa and Cyprus. On 23 March 1965 the Queen Mother visited the Centre. Parents attending were selected by random ballot. It was recorded that these included people not only from all regions of the British Isles, but also from India and Pakistan (before the creation of Bangladesh), Canada, Ghana, Nigeria and the Caribbean, from Italy, Poland, Cyprus and Switzerland.

In 1966 the Centre identified the needs of the immigrant populations. Poor housing and lack of provision and access to play and education for 2-5 year olds, were the most urgent health and welfare issues of the day. Poverty and discrimination meant that the Caribbeans were more disadvantaged than most.

An interesting insight into one of the problems of coping with this situation is that the staff and volunteers of Manor Gardens Centre found that it took a lot more time, per person, to deal with the new case load for cultural reasons. Even the most outgoing mother who could speak some British English as well as Caribbean English, and with a Christian upbringing, could take a little longer to explain her needs and understand the advice and requirement of a new social and health environment. At another 'extreme', if that may be allowed, might be the shy or culturally unconfident mother with little English and perhaps from a non-Christian background. In this respect some Cypriot families were at a disadvantage. One annual report even expresses some impatience with this.

So true to form the Centre started its own language classes to improve the standard of British English of parents. A slow start was made in 1971. By 1976 68 classes were held and there were 476 attendances. This became a wider form of cross-cultural socialising and parties with 'exotic food' were held. This was a peak however and by 1979 the numbers dropped to 37 classes and 104 attendances. As with many of the Centre's activities this was a timely response to an urgent need. The need either became less or was met by other providers, sometime in the statutory sector. Of course it does happen that some good projects are cut due to lack of or withdrawal of supporting funds, as we shall see later.

In the 2000s, following further immigration, often of refugees, for example from East Africa, the Middle East and Eastern Europe, the Centre responded with a Health Advocacy Service. This employed several hundred volunteers who were well educated, bilingual and able to act as advocates as well as being 'community interpreters' and guides to help new arrivals, who often had no previous British connections, to adapt to and find their way through the maze of the British health and welfare services. By this time there was a significant increase in the number of service users and volunteers of Islamic faith.

The Centre began to host a number of organisations set up to meet the needs of specific social and cultural groupings of refugees and recent immigrants. Others,

Prospective parents in the weighing room, 1960s.

A waiting room in the 1960s.

such as Age UK Islington and Islington Mind have dealt with such problems in a more generic fashion. The particular health need of a biologically specific population was addressed by the Centre's Sickle Cell Anaemia Counselling and Advisory Service in 1981. In the 1990s a Black and Ethnic Minority Health Project was active.

A notable event in the history of the Centre was a visit in 1969 by Archbishop Trevor Huddleston (1913-98). He worked as an Anglican priest amongst the poor of Johannesburg from 1943-56 when he was ordered back to London by his religious Order. He served as a Bishop in Tanzania (1960-68), Stepney (1968-78) and Mauritius (1978-83) becoming Archbishop of the Province of the Indian Ocean. A long time anti-apartheid activist, he became President of the Anti-Apartheid movement in 1981. He was a friend of Archbishop Tutu and many other activists. His book *Nought for your comfort* was widely read. There is still a youth centre in Hackney named after him. He was exceptionally well placed to advise and encourage the Centre at a time when Britain had become a highly diversified, multi-ethnic society and racism

Archbishop Trevor Huddleston, who visited the Centre in 1969.

was an even stronger threat to social harmony and order than today, not that it has disappeared. There is no substantial record of Trevor Huddleston's historic visit but it is clear that his counsel and words of wisdom, drawing on such depth of experience, made a strong and lasting impression. One of his key themes was the value of community spirit, including charitable action and volunteering. He was a strong critic of self-centred individualism on the one hand and bureaucratisation on the other. He had experienced far worse social conditions in Johannesburg and elsewhere, but he had found a strong community spirit in the poorer parts of London which was a value in itself as well as providing lifelines to those in greatest need.

Play and education for under-fives

The education as well as the health of young children and their mothers and fathers had been one of the main purposes of the Centre since its inauguration. In the first ten years the focus was on infants in their first year. Often it was first-time mothers who attended. But in any case they and others soon began to bring their sisters and brothers with them. Recall that five was the statutory age of the start of schooling, although not all children found a place immediately. So there was a need for at least what we would now call a 'crèche'.

The needs of 'toddlers' aged 1-5 became a matter of priority in its own right by the early 1920s. Mrs Leed's 'shelter', built on the side of No. 8, was designed to allow children to remain outside even in poor weather. Outdoors meant fresh air, sunlight, movement and interaction with other children. It was part of a holistic approach to human and personal development. Provision for this required chiefly the voluntary effort of mothers and others, who did not necessarily have any formal training or qualification. Toys and equipment were donated. Free milk began to be made available from the Council.

So in a sense play has been part of the Centre's curriculum and methodology from the beginning. So has recognition of the part played by play and early social education for the mental health and well-being of children. The 1977/78 annual report observes that:

'...there is evidence to show that many children who seemed in a fair way to becoming labelled 'backward' or 'difficult' or even 'sub-normal' were amenable to nothing more than imaginative care and commonsense and the freedom to move and mix and stretch themselves'.

The present thriving Manor Gardens Centre Pre-School developed out of these traditions and experiences.

In 1950 this aspect of our work was renewed and more firmly established. It was a field in which there was great need not filled by the NHS or other statutory provision. There were no local open spaces or parks. In 1950 Domini Crosfield donated money specifically to establish a new playroom, making better use of the garden space in front of the buildings. In 1952 it was noteworthy enough to be the subject of a feature in the *News Chronicle* daily newspaper. 'Toddlers' once again became prioritised and volunteers were called for, and were forthcoming. In 1955 the playroom was further improved and in that year 7,560 attendances by children recorded in the registers. The annual cost was £500.

In 1964 there were 14,000 attendances by children in the Playroom, as it was still known. The notion of 'guided play' appears in the record. In 1967 the Princess Elizabeth Hall was for the first time redesignated and devoted to a space for a 'Play Centre', becoming a more organised 'Playgroup' in 1969 with 15-20 children attending each session. The key mover and Head of the Pre-School was Anne Jennings, who engaged, as did others following her example, in further study to gain qualifications necessary in this increasingly important area of education. She

Playgroup activities in the 1970s.

The Queen Mother, with Anne Jennings, at a Play Group in 1988.

was in charge of the Playgroup and Pre-School for a total of forty years. She welcomed the Queen Mother on the occasion of her visit in 1988. By 1982 the Playgroup became known as the 'Pre-School Play Group' and now as the 'Pre-School'. An early supervisor of the playroom was Mrs Cynthia Landeryou who also served on the Executive Committee and did much else for the Centre as a volunteer from 1953 up to 1999. She started a link with BBC's Children in Need Appeal which continues to this day.

Governance 1948-77

For most of our existence the Centre has been governed by an Executive Committee with an average of twelve members, chaired by a senior person often for a long period. Thus Domini Crosfield was our Chairman from 1919-1959. There were no rules about length of tenure. The Chair was active and played a key public role. The task of executive officer or chief administrator was undertaken by the Honorary Secretary, thus Florence Keen 1913-1937, Althea Davis (née Keen) 1947-75.

Florence Keen, after her death and for many years was listed as Founder. The titles President and Vice-President have been used intermittently as honorific titles, usually to honour and maintain a link with outgoing Chairs and Hon. Secretaries. In recent years this usage has lapsed.

The practice of having a General Committee wider than the Executive was designed to allow the participation of ex officio members and other supernumeraries. All the Executive Committee were members of the General Committee, which was rather cumbersome. This fell out of use after 1948. Subsequently the Executive Committee sometimes included elected Council members but not Council officials. Of note were: Elizabeth Hoodless from 1966, and Milton Baballul and Stephen Twigg (1992-96). In some notable cases the distinguished husbands of our senior members also joined the Committee: Sir Alexander Maxwell, Sir Mark Turner and Lord Brimelow.

Boy in Play Group, 1980s.

Boy in Pre-School 2010.

NHS AND AFTER – A KIND OF INDEPENDENCE

The Centre has been a registered Charity with a Board of Trustees since 1925. At first when there were still legal restrictions on women's participation in such matters, the Board usually consisted of three men, sometimes all or mostly members of the family and in any case people with qualifications in accountancy, audit and the role of Treasurer. The Trustees' work is seldom referred to in annual reports and seems to have played a low profile role providing the minimum legal requirement for financial oversight and audit. It is not until the 1990s, as we shall see that the role of the Trustees began to be radically transformed.

During the period 1947-75 the Centre was largely managed by Althea Davis whom we have introduced, with the support of Lady Peggy Turner who was our Chairman from 1960-77. Lady Turner had joined the Committee in 1956. Her husband Sir Mark Turner was on the Committee from 1959-77. He had worked with Aneurin Bevan in the Ministry of Economic Warfare. After the war he became chairman of British Home Stores and then Rio Tinto Zinc.

As we have seen the 1970s were years of decline in many respects. Althea Davis resigned in 1975, becoming President. In 1977 there was a brief period of crisis when the Centre had neither an Honorary Secretary nor a Chairman. Althea had to come out of retirement to edit the annual report. A temporary administrator was employed for about a year. We eventually found a new Chairman who was to help us transform the fortunes of the Manor Gardens Centre.

PART SIX

Renewal and Transformation

Voluntary Action

The case for the value of voluntary action in community health and welfare began to be more carefully and cogently argued in the twentieth century in parallel with the continuous, and soon large-scale, increase in state provision. One of the earliest contributions to this debate was the *Minority Report of the Poor Law Commission 1906-9* for which Beatrice and Sydney Webb were largely responsible. They adduced strong arguments for voluntary agencies.

The next milestones were Lord Beveridge's reports on voluntary action (especially that of 1948), and a timely intervention by Richard Crossman in a paper on 'The role of the volunteer in the modern social service' in 1976 which was closely followed by the recommendations of Lord Wolfenden's committee on the future of voluntary organisations.

William Beveridge had a career that resembled in many ways those of other social reformers and philanthropists who have been part of our story. He was a warden at Toynbee Hall and a Professor of Economics at the London School of Economics, of which he became Director from 1919-37. He is best known for the 'Beveridge Plan' of 1942 which led the way to the welfare state. He was influenced by Fabian socialism but later became a Liberal. He showed interest in the eugenics movement, particularly in his proposal to correct the declining birth rate by encouraging professional classes to have more children than poorer households by means of a discriminatory state allowance. In his report of 1948 he says:

> *'Time after time philanthropy [voluntary action] is seen breaking in on official routine, unveiling evils, finding fresh channels for service, getting things done that would not be done for pay.'*

John Wolfenden (1906-85) was an educationalist, probably best remembered for his influential report recommending the decriminalisation of homosexuality in 1957. He was appointed in 1974 to chair a committee of enquiry into the future of voluntary organisations. The report, published in 1978, set agendas for the next twenty-five years, the period of the 'revival' of the Manor Gardens Centre.

The report had two main concerns:

Annual gathering of Volunteers and presentation of awards for service by Jeremy Corbyn,
MP for Islington North 1983-.

a) the need to strengthen and extend collective action;
b) the need to ensure a pluralistic style of provision and power.

The report looks at a wide range of voluntary action in the context of what is done respectively in state, commercial and 'informal' sectors. It deals chiefly with national scale voluntary organisations and local authorities. Islington is shown to have a comparatively good record.

The report sees the chief forms of action of voluntary organisations as:

a) acting as pressure groups to change policies and provision;
b) pioneering new services;
c) providing complementary, additional or alternative services;
d) acting as sole provider of certain services.

The key principles and aims are: independence, responsibility and effectiveness.

The Geraldine Aves watershed 1977-80

Watershed is a big word. But if we were at a low ebb by 1977 we were soon launched on a new tide of activity with enthusiasm which changed the course of our history. The appointment of Dame Geraldine Maitland Aves as our new Chairman in 1977 was the key that unlocked this floodgate. In her Younghusband Lecture of 1983 Dame Geraldine referred to the Centre in the 1970s as being 'in the doldrums', which sounds like a polite understatement. She also refers to its being 'rescued' and 'new life put into it'.

Dame Geraldine Aves DBE 1898-1986

Geraldine Aves was a retired senior civil servant and social reformer. She was a person of great strength and independence of mind. The author of her biography, Phyllis Willmott (a member of the Executive Committee) characterises her as 'an authoritative persona, touched with charisma'. *The Times* obituarist said that an 'enthusiasm for unorthodox ideas and social experiment were the hallmarks of her approach'. Unlike most of Florence Keen's generation of upper class ladies she had gone to University – read economics at Newnham College, Cambridge – and had then taken up a full-time career, rising to the top of her profession. Having distinguished herself running the LCC's School Care services, she was given charge of plans for the evacuation of families from London (1938-41) and later the welfare of people using public air raid shelters.. She moved to the Ministry of Health in 1942 and became Head of the Welfare Division. Her work took on international dimensions working for the United Nations Family and Child Welfare Division and the United Nations Relief and Rehabilitation Administration in Europe (UNRRA).

From 1965-72 Geraldine Aves, now CBE, was Chair of 'The National Corporation for the care of Old People' and most importantly she chaired the committee of enquiry which produced the Aves *Report on the Voluntary Worker in the Social Services.*

Dame Geraldine Aves DBE, 1898-1986.

Following this, shortly before joining Manor Gardens Centre, she founded 'The Volunteer Centre', a national body that supported volunteer recruitment and training. For these contributions she was created Dame of the Order of the British Empire (DBE) in 1977.

Like her biographer, Phyllis Willmott, and so many of our leading figures, she was a resident of Highgate. Her sister was married to David Waterlow, son of Sir Sydney Waterlow, benefactor of Waterlow Park. Her father had worked at Toynbee Hall where he was a good friend of Charles Booth and was his co-worker. Geraldine founded the Harrington Society in Highgate for children with learning difficulties.

A major review

Dame Geraldine immediately set up a working group to consider 'ways in which the Centre might develop its work in the light of local needs'. It made three major recommendations:

1. to appoint a full-time Centre Co-ordinator;
2. to work more closely with the Borough Social Welfare Department;
3. to make better use of our premises.

In 1979 Mr Brian Earl was appointed Centre Co-ordinator. He was energetic, hands-on in management style, imaginative and well liked. He lived in a small flat on the premises. He developed and implemented many new plans and projects that have had a lasting effect to this day. He researched new income streams and potential projects. He helped to set up a second Trust to cover the new range of activities. Some relatively minor changes are nonetheless symptomatic of the new and optimistic mood. The Centre became known as The Manor Gardens Centre for the first time in 1979. This reflected 'a widening of the aims of the Trust to meet the changing needs of a modern society'. The cover of the annual report was changed from 1980/81. It then used an image of the Centre buildings for several years before going 'freestyle' as now. It lost the image of a loosely clad infant taken from a plaster 'tondo' or roundel that was formerly fixed to the wall by the entrance. Unlike the three dimensional image, the logo had the Latin motto *Dat Deus Incrementum* (God gives us increase). The brickwork of the buildings, which had once been almost covered with ivy, was cleaned.

The Centre's Annual Report for 1986, the year Dame Geraldine died aged 88, recorded this in recognition of her major role:

'[She] became responsible for encouraging the Executive Committee to respond to modern day needs. She helped us, indeed forced us, to move in new directions and to recapture our pioneering reputation. She was instrumental in encouraging small voluntary organisations to become established here giving rise to the unusual mixture of practical services housed at Manor Gardens Centre.'

The Dame Geraldine watershed is also marked by the upturn in our rate of expenditure and corresponding funding.

The first years' turnover reflect the beginnings of the Aves watershed effect:

1977/8	£34,103	(£3,254 deficit)
1978/9	£43,938	(£11,411 deficit)
1979/80	£45,229	(no deficit)

Finances are discussed further below. To anticipate, the comparable figure for 2011/12 was £1,637,000.

Women and the Centre

We have already noted the predominant part played by women in the Manor Gardens Centre story. For the first two-thirds of the first century this was the prevailing pattern. All the senior roles were played by women: Patron, President, Chair, Doctors and Nurses. The men involved were of several categories. First, there were the accountants and lawyers who acted as Trustees. They included Florence Keen's husband and son, followed by the son of a longstanding female volunteer. Secondly, there were a few dentists as this service developed. Thirdly, there was a small number of men who served ex officio on the General Committee, such as the Medical Officer of Health. Fourthly, were the husbands of the women who brought their children to the clinics and often stayed as volunteers. These were the members of the Fathers Committee and their friends and helpers. Finally, there were usually one or two 'handymen' or janitors. In later years a number of distinguished husbands of the senior women joined the committee or the Board of Trustees, usually after their retirement from senior public office.

Brian Earl, appointed in January 1979, was our first paid, full-time senior administrator. This heralded a period in which some senior offices, both paid and voluntary, were held by men. Women have tended to continue to figure largely among the leaders and managers of our service projects. Men play an increasing role among volunteers. On the whole we might say that we have gone some way to create a balanced gender profile in the Centre at all levels of responsibility, but with women continuing to be the majority.

The last thirty years have also seen a steady increase in the numbers of staff, trustees and especially volunteers from what are currently known as 'black and minority ethnic groups'. These changes, both in gender and ethnic origin are worthy of further monitoring and research.

Governance and management from 1980

Dame Geraldine had made it clear when appointed that she would serve a limited time. This was to be four full years and the impact, and the reverberations of what she had started with Brian Earl's help had a much longer life. As a small token we named the newly refurbished building at the eastern end of our estate The Dame Geraldine Hall.

In May 1981 the Chairmanship passed to Mrs Mana Sedgwick OBE, JP, who served for three years. She was followed in turn by Mrs Caroline Osborn (1984-89) with Tim Davis, son of Althea Davis, as Vice-Chair. Caroline Osborn had been Chair of the Working Party for the Elderly of the Community Health Council, based at the Whittington Hospital. Caroline Osborn was a Quaker, married to Derek Osborn a senior civil servant in the Department of the Environment and later Vice-Chair of the Institute of International Environmental Development. She encouraged Jane Lethbridge, who had served also on the Community Health Council, to succeed her as Chair of the Manor Gardens Executive Committee

In 1986 Robert Warner, Tim Davis' son-in-law, and newly qualified accountant, joined the Committee as Treasurer. He was to serve for over thirty years until 2007.

Brian Earl resigned in 1987 to resume a career in teaching in the north of England. The position of Director was filled by Laura MacGillivray. She was young, ambitious and highly effective. The annual report said of her at her resignation: 'she undertook enormous administrative re-organisation, set in motion many important project initiatives and re-established a forward looking, dynamic Centre'. She continued the momentum set in motion by her predecessor. She was however a more modern office administrator, more systematic, and introduced the beginnings of computerisation. She left in May 1990. She is currently Chief Executive Officer of Norwich City Council. There were to be two other Directors in the 1990s: Teresa Bednall (1990-96) and Amelia Curwen (1996-1999).

The external environment in which the Centre worked underwent some important changes in the period 1980-2000. The Camden and Islington Area Health Authority had been set up in 1979 transformed in 1996 to become the Camden and Islington Health Service. Early in the 1980s plans started to be made for the transfer of NHS functions carried out on the Manor Gardens site, to the Royal Northern

Laura MacGillivray, Director 1988-91.

Hospital. This was closed in 1984 but the original hospital building was converted into a multi-purpose health centre for a large GP practice and a variety of other services. The last of the Council NHS services left the Centre in 2001.

It has always been our experience that just as you think you have reached a new plateau of achievement, new foothills and then mountain ranges loom, new challenges to surmount. When Frank Wood became our Director in 2000 he found much to do. He was our most experienced Director to date. He had a career in management with British Telecom (formerly General Post Office) and had changed careers to become Deputy Director of the St Margaret's House Settlement in Bethnal Green, and so had experience in both the public and voluntary sectors. The governance and financial management of the Centre were the main issues. Many trustees and committee members had been serving for a very long time, a practice discouraged by the Charity Commissioners. The Chair had been part of the team for some forty years. He took his role seriously and visited the Centre once in between each quarterly meeting, but it was hard for him, to say the least, to keep in touch with what was going on in Islington and the field of community health and welfare.

We had no full-time finance manager. We employed a financial consultant, John Blackwood, who visited once a week and trained a staff member who had no previous qualification in this field. Frank Wood took the earliest opportunity to appoint a full-time finance manager, William Meghoma in November 2004, now Finance Director, who is still with us in 2013.

The infrastructure was another issue. Boilers had not been serviced; some of the electrical wiring was over 60 years old; no fire drills had been carried out for some years. Some of these conditions were no doubt in breach of regulations, and Frank Wood dealt with them with due urgency. He conducted a full survey and set up a programme of on-going maintenance.

The Centre's own projects were flourishing, but the long anticipated withdrawal of all NHS services, that had been with us for fifty years, finally became a reality. The NHS had rented more than twenty rooms. At one time they managed the whole of the reception area; at another they shared it with the Centre. They tended therefore, even if unintentionally, to be predominant in the public perception of what the Manor Gardens Centre stood for as a Charity. Most of their services, including speech therapy, podiatry, family planning and health visitors, moved to the new Northern Medical Centre in the remaining part of the old Royal Northern Hospital. Some people thought at the time that this might be the end of the Centre. In a way it clarified and strengthened our independence and resolve. The NHS parted on good terms, even contributing £40,000 towards refurbishment of the premises they had occupied. This and the fact that Frank Wood soon managed to find alternative tenants for all these rooms without loss of rental income, is greatly to his credit.

Finances and financial management

The tradition of seeking and receiving privately donated funds continued even though our principal funders were public authorities. For example in 1979 and 1998, as it had on previous occasions, Channing Girls School made collections for the Centre. Previous and current trustees, officers and volunteers continued to donate. The Queen Mother donated £500 on the occasion of her Jubilee in 1987. Even the Leverhulme estate continued to donate at its original rate until at least 1991. Various banks, the Stock Exchange and City funds made their contributions, and there were always surprises and very welcome new donors, such as the Arsenal Football Club.

The Centre's 'turnover', based on annual expenditure, has risen from £235 in our first year (about £12-15,000 in today's terms) to approximately £1,700,000 at the end of our century. We built up rapidly during the First World War and by 1921 our expenditure was £6,580 (say £330,000 - 400,000 in today's terms). There was a slight dip in the first years of the Second World War, then recovery and some progress, but, given low inflation the totals remained rather similar until the mid-1950s. The subsequent increases reflect inflation as much as increased activity.

The Centre has always been well

The Annual Report for 1914.

North Islington School for Mothers.

FIRST ANNUAL REPORT,
1914.

NORTH ISLINGTON
INFANT WELFARE CENTRE
& SCHOOL FOR MOTHERS

OPENED IN 1913

SIXTY-FOURTH
ANNUAL REPORT
1976 - 77

6-9 MANOR GARDENS
HOLLOWAY ROAD, N7 6LA

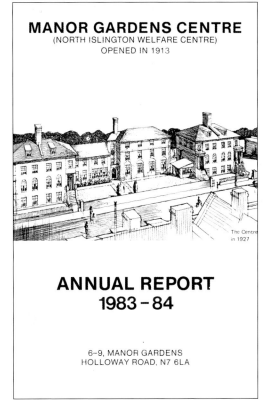

MANOR GARDENS CENTRE
(NORTH ISLINGTON WELFARE CENTRE)
OPENED IN 1913

The Centre
in 1927

ANNUAL REPORT
1983 – 84

6–9, MANOR GARDENS
HOLLOWAY ROAD, N7 6LA

The Annual Report 1976-77   *The Annual Report 1983-84*

served by those responsible for its financial affairs. For a great many years our treasurers, auditors and financial managers have been volunteers. At first Mr William Brock Keen, who was head of a large practice of City accountants, was a Trustee. His son Hugh Keen, also an accountant, took over, retiring after the Second World War after a break for service in the RAF. Mr Alan Fabes provided continuity of service as accountant and then treasurer from 1942 until he was replaced as Treasurer by Florence Keen's grandson-in-law Robert Warner, an accountant in 1985. Shortly before he resigned from the Board in 2007, the current Finance Director, William Meghoma had been appointed. Excellent accounts have been presented at each AGM and printed in the Annual Report. A detailed examination of the Centre's financial history lies beyond the scope of this book, but would repay further research. Over many years the Centre's reputation for financial accountability and probity has encouraged our supporters to continue funding us over a period of years.

As mentioned earlier the Centre has never had sufficient capital to invest in endowment funds or stocks and shares. On the other hand, prudent management and accounting have meant that we have seldom had an end of year deficit. There were deficits in three consecutive years in 1977, 1978 and 1979 peaking at £11,411 or a third of the previous year's expenditure. But these were the years of an extension of activities, and consequently turnover increased considerably year on year. It has been difficult to build up any reserve funds from surpluses. This difficulty is common enough in small to medium sized charities especially when income is largely for tightly costed budgets for specific services. There is currently an urgent need to increase our income for capital developments and for building up reserves, especially from donations to a general fund.

In 1996 the 'contract culture' was first noted in the annual report. This was the new preference for competitive bidding for 'service level agreement' contracts to supply services to local health and welfare authorities, especially the Primary Care Trusts, usually for no more than three years, and not always renewed. This had a negative effect on the philanthropic support for the Centre. Since recent changes in government policy from 2010, with cuts in the budgets of the commissioning authorities, it has become necessary for organisations such as ours to revive the role of private funding for specific and general funding purposes.

Following Dame Geraldine's guidance the rational and financially optimal use of the space available on the Manor Gardens Centre estate was radically re-examined. The meant chiefly the potential rental value for offices and meetings and activity spaces. Since the 1980s the rental income from charitable organisations sharing our space has been a crucially valuable income stream.

An important opportunity for expanding our space and resource base for our projects occurred when the GPO building was converted into more than 400 private dwellings, owned leasehold. It is now known as the Beaux-Arts Building after a style of European architecture current at the time it was built in 1911. In 1997, under a planning regulation known as 'Section 106', the ground floor and basement of No. 10 Manor Gardens, an annexe of the main building consisting of 557.4 square metres or 6,000 square feet on two floors, was rented to the Manor Gardens Centre at a 'peppercorn rent' for a period of 30 years, renewable only for community use.

The Manor Gardens Centre only invites and accepts organisations, whether large or small, which not only have charitable status - this much is required by the Charities Law - but whose purposes and practice are in harmony with our own. Two of the largest and longest dwelling residents have been Islington Mind and Age UK Islington. It has long been the hope that this community of users will be just that, a friendly and co-operative community that can add up to more than the sum of its parts. The potential of creating a truly integrated campus, identifying common interests and synergies, and developing joint initiatives are great indeed and much has to be done to develop this more fully.

One of the tenant organisations we are particularly proud of is the Women's Therapy Centre. It was founded in 1976 by Dr Susie Orbach and Dr Luise Eichenbaum, feminist psychotherapists who had worked together for some years in America in the early 1970s. They saw the Centre as part of the Women's Movement. It has continued to provide services for adult women by women professionals. The current Chief Executive is Ann Byrne, who has held the post for some twelve years.

One of her predecessors was Linda Massie who came to them after working with Islington Mind at the Manor Gardens Centre. Linda Massie's MA thesis on the first ten years of the North Islington Welfare Centre was discussed earlier *(see section on Racism and Eugenics above)*.

An average 60 'occasional users' rent space during the year for meetings, seminars, training sessions etc.

Services provided from 1977

A recurring theme in this account has been the emphasis on a holistic approach to health and wellbeing. Our initial focus on 'Infant Welfare' and a 'School for Mothers' may look quite specialised but it developed rapidly into services for toddlers and then older children, with increasing attention paid to their mothers' needs, before and after childbirth. The scope was widened to include advice and training in parenting, coping with living conditions, budgeting, dieting, referral and access to public services and increasing opportunities to benefit directly from, for example, massage, physical exercise, classes for clothes making and cookery, and having a family holiday. In times of war bereavement counselling, as we now call it, added another dimension. Home helps, and the possibility of spending a week or more in residence with babies in the Wards, gave mothers an element of respite. Social gatherings were held and the kitchen never ceased to cater for a range of purposes.

We need to bear this in mind when talking about the large range and number of services that we see coming on stream after the late 1970s, the final third of our first century. Some are clearly continuations of original services, suitably transformed and up-dated, notably the Play Group, now the Pre-School, and the kitchen function. Some are to do with quite new demographics. When we started the great issue was infant mortality with a death rate in Islington of 150 per thousand and life expectancy was about 50 (nationally 53.4). Now this has 'reversed' so to say. The infant death rate is approximately 3-4 per thousand, chiefly in the first few weeks. Life expectancy (2010) for men is 75 and women 81, both a little below national average. This is a staggering difference which suggests some form of social progress.

Another demographic change has been the increase in numbers of people, first, second and third generation, who have backgrounds in other countries, notably the Commonwealth. Many of these are now part of 'mixed race' families, to use the preferred self-designation. Thus, as stated earlier, we have addressed the particular health and welfare needs of African-Caribbean people; we have provided language classes and health advocacy services to support newcomers and help them participate more easily as new citizens. The serious issue of FGM (female genital mutilation) is currently being addressed. First generation newcomers are more prone to suffer from diseases we had thought eradicated in this country, such as TB and rickets.

Some issues were relatively 'taboo' in our early days. These include for example, family planning (contraception), sexual health of young people, gay and lesbian rights and advisory groups, and child abuse. There are also less 'visible' issues such as victim support, social isolation and agoraphobia.

Just as our founders responded to innovative ideas, many of the changes of emphasis discussed here, and what seems like a proliferation of specialised services, result from new kinds of socio-political thinking from the 1960s onwards, and from important advances in theory and practice of new forms of therapy.

Many themes and issues cross cut and overlap between projects and this offers opportunities for synergies. For example: mental wellbeing, social isolation and volunteering (training). The style of work or nature of 'delivery' of services includes advice and referral, counselling, training, therapy, personal friendship and mentoring, campaigning, and whenever possible enabling and empowering.

Here is a partial list of services offered at the Manor Gardens Centre in recent years (both own projects and those of resident organisations). Some are current, some have lasted many years. Some alas have had to be curtailed in their prime due to lack of financial support. There are of course some overlaps between the broad categories used.

Services for infants, young children and families
Play Group, then Pre-School
Toy Library
Language Delay Unit
Speech Therapy
Family Welfare Association
Midwives Clinic
Carers Project
Family Planning
Family Rights
Accident Prevention Loan Scheme
Parents Anonymous (battered children)
Gingerbread (single parent families)

Services for teenagers and young adults
London Teenage Gay Group
Asian Girls Group
Brook Advisory Clinic (sexual health, to age 25)
Youth Club
Baobab Centre(for survivors of extreme violence, trafficking and rape)

Services for Adults
Stroke Club
Women's Therapy
Health Advocacy Project
Mental Health Champions Project
Islington Mind

Above, the Queen Mother visits the Lunch Club in 1988. Below, Reuben helping lunch club member.

Work with disabled young adults was a priority in the 1980s and 1990s. They went to Moscow on an exchange and made a film in Tenerife.

Black and Ethnic Minority Health Project
Sickle Cell Anaemia
NACRO (rehabilitation of offenders)
Islington Peoples Rights
Keep Fit/ Slimming
Bereavement Counselling
Agoraphobics Group
Music for All
Victims Support Group

Services for Older People
Pensioner Link
Geriatric Health Circle
Lunch Club
Chiropody
Befriending and Respite Scheme
Friendship Telephone Network
AGLOW (London older women's group)
Age UK Islington

Country and ethnic group associations

Carila (Portuguese and Spanish speakers)

Shanti

African Sub Saharan Development Partnership

African Relief Support Project

African Women and Children Support Organisation

B2B Somali Arts and Education Ltd.

Congolese Association of Elderly People

Other

Kitchen (Community Kitchens Project, Healthy Eating, Café)

Ambulance Service

Charity Shop

Left: Festival of wellbeing.

Below: Respite and Befriending Project 2009.

Community Kitchens Project 2008.

Two case studies
The Stroke Project

The Stroke Project was started in July 1980. It has been the longest lasting of the new projects initiated after Brian Earl's arrival in 1979. It has had only two managers during this time: Gillian Young (1980-98) and Kath Birkett (1998-present).

The Project provides a rehabilitation and social facility for people who have had strokes. It aims to improve the quality of life and empower people to take greater responsibility for themselves. This has been achieved by means of exercise, physiotherapy, T'ai Chi, Yoga, dance, excursions, hydrotherapy and other less physical means such as singing, computer use and aromatherapy. People with limited mobility or speech, even those who thought they perhaps were likely to be forever confined to a wheelchair, become more able to move with growing confidence. People who thought their speech or ability to write would not recover are able to increase their powers of communication. Training and therapy, together with socialising with people in similar, or worse, situations, helps to increase self-respect and reduce social isolation, anxiety and depression.

The scheme has a preventative purpose too. It has organised workshops on healthy lifestyles in Schools and Community Groups, in order to explain some of the origins of strokes and cardiovascular disorders and means of avoiding them.

At the core of activity is the 'Stroke Club' which meets twice a week from 10.00 am to 3.30 pm in the Dame Geraldine Aves Hall and once a week in the south of the borough at St Luke's Centre. This provides an occasion for a shared meal, which can be a learning experience in itself. The Club has 30 or more members at any time, and it is very much 'owned' by them. The majority of members are over 60 years old, but younger adults also participate.

Not all people are able to get to the Centre, so there is an outreach service to visit them at home. Information packs and one-to-one advice are offered to all members of the wider circle and their carers. Advice and information includes advocacy in matters of public welfare benefits, referrals to other services, and a

ИСПОЛНИТЕЛЬНЫЙ КОМИТЕТ ОРДЕНА ЛЕНИНА
СОЮЗА ОБЩЕСТВ КРАСНОГО КРЕСТА И КРАСНОГО ПОЛУМЕСЯЦА СССР
(СОКК и КП СССР)

117036, Москва, Черемушкинский проезд, 5. Телефон 126-57-51. Телеграф Москва — ПКРЕСТПОЛ

21.03.91 № 240/1627

На № ——————— от ——————

Mrs. Laura McGillivray,

Director,
MANOR GARDENS CENTRE
6-9 Manor Gardens, Holloway Road
London N7 6LA
U.K.

Dear Laura,

Thank you very much for your letter of February 22,1991. We are sorry that the trip of your group was postponed, but we hope that we will have a possibility to meet you in the Soviet Union in future.

All the members of our delegation, visited Manor Gardens last July, want to express feelings of gratitude for your hospitality and cordiality. We will be glad to accept a group from Manor Gardens at any convenient time, but please inform us in advance about the visit.

Dear Laura, as you are leaving the post of the Director of Manor Gardens, we would like to remind you that you are always welcome in the Soviet Union, maybe colleagues from your new job will be interested in developing good relations with Soviet Red Cross and Moscow organisation of disabled people.

We will be happy to see you in the Soviet Union.

Best regards from Dr.A.Tretyakov, Head of International Cooperation Department of the Soviet Red Cross.

Sincerely,

21.03.91

Galina Shakhova,
Senior Officer, International Cooperation Dept
Soviet Red Cross

117036, USSR, Moscow
1 Tcheremushkinski proezd, 5
International Cooperation Dept
of the Soviet Red Cross

Letter from the Russian Red Cross, 1991.

Telephone Friend 2009.

service to provide intensive support in particular crises. For many years the work of the Project was made easier by use of the Centre's own bus/ambulance and its capable drivers. This service eventually proved uneconomical and was cut, but fortunately other special transport services have taken its place and many members are now mobile by using their electric 'scooters' to get to the Centre.

For as long as the Centre operated its own bus, the project had a long-standing relationship with Pentonville Prison which enabled members to use the Prison gymnasium and hydrotherapy pool, helped by professional and prison volunteers. In addition to classes in the various skills and therapies listed above, some activities of members over the years have included: visits to the seaside at Southend, visits to Kew Gardens and Kenwood House, the Islington Boat Club and tea dances at Caxton House.

Recent members' comments include the following:

'If I didn't come here I'd have nowhere to go. It's good for me to talk and get things done that I couldn't otherwise do.'

'The Stroke Club listened and helped me to cope.'

'Services and care offered by workers are excellent. It provides several forms of rehabilitation facilities.'

Volunteers, as in all Projects and activities, have been crucial to the success of the Stroke Project. Some helpers are people who have had strokes themselves. Each year there may be 20-30 or more volunteers working with the Project.

Another valuable dimension to the work has been involvement by senior students from various nearby institutions and authorities. These included a long-standing relation with the University of North London (London Metropolitan

University) which has sent students on placements or internships. In the past ten years numbers of students attending were:

Medical	319
Nursing	87
Social Work	81
Social Care	15
Work placements	2

This brief case study illustrates so many of the features of the work of the Centre and what it stands for that it is a good moment to look at the guiding principles, values and priorities. They will of course be referred to again in specific contexts.

1. We respond to local need for health and social care that is not being addressed or fully met elsewhere.
2. We aim to promote health as a counterbalance to orthodox emphasis on diseases, other extreme conditions and their cures.
3. We offer services to those most disadvantaged.
4. We do not discriminate in terms of gender, age, ethnicity, religion or lifestyle.
5. We offer friendly, caring, holistic and wherever possible one-to-one services.
6. We prioritise learning and enabling, understanding of causes and prevention.
7. We aim to reduce social isolation and exclusion.

Stroke Club members 1987

8   We address, as part of any project, issues of mental wellbeing, reduction of anxiety and depression, loneliness and low self-esteem.

9   We address the concerns of new communities and new citizens including refugees and asylum seekers.

10   We seek to develop partnerships with sponsors, local authorities, educational institutions and community groups.

11   We aim to attract and recruit volunteers and to provide access to approved training as well as work experience, to enable career development.

12   We aim to contribute, within our field of competence, to

Above, Gillian Young, first manager of the Stroke Project. Below, Stroke Club member and Volunteer.

Above. Stroke Club exercises 2008.

Left: Kath Birkett, Stroke Cub Manager, 2012.

the national system of education and qualification, such as Key Stages 3, 4 and 5, NVQs, degrees and other professional qualifications.

Almost all of the aims and priorities listed are 'generic', in that they can and do apply to any or all of our undertakings. Obviously each Project has a primary focus, but in measuring 'outcomes' and assessing capabilities and successes generally it is important to bear in mind this large raft of 'added values'. Much of what is achieved is not clearly visible; it lies below the waterline. It is far from a matter of simply showing 'service delivered'. The whole is more than the sum of its parts. This is what the Centre means by claiming to provide services of the highest quality.

Health Advocacy Project

The Health Advocacy Project is a more recent member of the Manor Gardens Centre team. It was started in 1998. Its first manager was Marsha Saunders, followed by Sam Page and since 2007 Hekate Papadaki. It has been funded by Islington PCT and for three or four years also by Camden PCT and the European Social Fund.

Its purpose, as defined in a statement in 2010 is 'to ensure equal rights for disadvantaged Black and Minority Ethnic, Refugee and Asylum Seeking communities in Islington, neighbouring boroughs and the wider London area'. Even more specifically 'to achieve this through Bilingual Advocacy and Health Services as well as Health Education initiatives'.

As with the stroke project the immediate focus is clear and simple: enabling access to health services: GPs, local hospitals and other clinics and service providers. In practice however the service becomes a much broader and deeper involvement in the members' lives and their experiences of being newcomers to this country. There are often preceding and underlying traumas, complex familial arrangements and cultural issues, multiple needs across the health and social services sectors.

The case notes of the advocates reveal the depth and complexity of their work. Naima, a volunteer interpreter and advocate for the Health Advocacy Project, was interpreting for an appointment with a new female client, Ms K, at a GP surgery. Ms K said she felt depressed and was unhappy with her life. After a few more appointments, Ms K begun to trust Naima and revealed that she and her nine-year old daughter were experiencing domestic violence from her husband. The daughter herself had phoned the police but as Ms K did not speak English, she was unclear what the police had understood or what her daughter had been able to convey. Ms K told Naima that whenever she talked of leaving her husband, he threatened to keep their two children, and send her back to Syria (her country of origin). She was extremely worried that this would happen as her residency depended on her marriage. In the past, the husband had always accompanied Ms K to the GP so she was unable seek help.

Through the Advocacy Project, Ms K was referred to Solace Women's Aid. As there were only 30 minutes each day when Ms K was without her husband, it was agreed that Naima would complete an initial in-depth referral form with Ms K by phone during this time-slot. Ms K trusted Naima, and felt more confident to reveal the further details of her case. She also asked Naima to accompany her to her next GP appointment and to inform the GP what was happening. Naima arranged with the domestic violence worker to meet Ms K at her women's exercise class which she attended on her own once a week. Immediately after referral and assessment Ms K and her children were moved to a safe house in a different borough and the children were moved to a different school. Ms K told us 'Naima has saved me from my awful life and I can now see a future for myself and my children.'

Above, Health Advocacy Project training seminarr.
Below, Hekate Papadaki, Health Advocacy Project Manager, 2012.

As the Project has developed, new issues and new ways of working have emerged. It holds workshops for community groups on mental wellbeing, substance abuse, screening, healthy living and protection from abuse. Recently the issue of Female Genital Mutilation has been taken up by the Project with funding support from The Trust for London and the Esmée Fairbairn Foundation. Educative workshops on the subject are being delivered to teachers, social workers and care professionals not only in Islington but also in neighbouring boroughs of Haringey and Hackney. In 2010/11 347 people were supported within this initiative. Other local partnerships have been made with the Whittington Hospital, the African Well Women's Centre and the City and Islington College.

In 2011 the project delivered mental wellbeing workshops for women from Arabic, Kurdish and Somali communities, and one on TB for the Somali community.

As ever the scheme can only work with the help of volunteers, of whom there have been several hundred in the past few years. All are at least bilingual, speaking one or more of the twenty or so languages preponderant among the members, particularly from the Horn of Africa, Francophone Africa, the Middle East and Eastern Europe. Languages currently in demand include: Amharic, Arabic, Bengali, Dari, Farsi, Kurdish, Polish, Pushtu, Russian, Somali, Tigrigna and Turkish. Some volunteers are well-qualified professionals in their own countries. Many have themselves endured the same terrible experiences of their clients.

A parallel aim of the Health Advocacy Project is to recruit, train and support the team of Health Advocates. In 2009 this aim was elaborated as follows: 'to improve the employability of refugees through providing robust training and vocational education programmes in Community Interpreting and Bi-lingual Health Advocacy as well as voluntary and work experience opportunities'. In 2010 31 volunteers completed accredited training and to date 58% have found paid employment as a result of the 'stepping stone' to employment offered by the Project. One volunteer commented:

'The training, development and on-going support that Manor Gardens provides to community members are invaluable. It boosts the confidence of trainees and equips them with essential knowledge to help the most disadvantaged members of their communities. The project is playing a vital role in making a difference to the lives of volunteers (like me).'

Chris O'Kane, Head of Pre-School, 2012.

The Board of Trustees

In 1985 the Board had only four members: Tim Davis, Alan Fabes, Robert Warner and Lady Brimelow. In 1988 the Centre had an Executive Committee, a Finance Committee reinstituted after a great many years, and a Board of Trustees. Tim Davis later renamed the Executive Committee the Management Committee. This combination proved not to be a sustainable arrangement. Tim Davis was Chairman of the Executive Committee, a restoration of the Keen family connection. He was also Chairman of the Board of Trustees. The Board of Trustees gradually became his preferred instrument of governance. By the early 2000s the Board became the sole means of governance. Tim Davis was the adopted son of Althea Davis. He was a prosperous farmer in Oxfordshire and one-time President of the National Farmers' Union. He was a traditionalist, arch-loyal to what he saw as his family's original mission. So much so that late in his time of office, when he realised how far the Centre had developed from being mainly to do with mothers and their infants, he proposed handing over the whole of the Charity's assets to Dr Barnados in the mid-1990s.

A notable achievement was the formation of a single Trust, The Manor Gardens Welfare Trust, as it remains to the present. There had previously been two charities: the North Islington Welfare Centre, a derivative of the original trust, and The Manor Gardens Community Trust that had been added as we expanded our role. When Tim Davis retired in 2002 after forty-four years of service, there had already been a hand-over of the post of Director to Frank Wood. Several changes in governance and management ensued. Management and Trustees undertook a thorough review of governance, human resources and other equal opportunities policies were updated and many other procedures, self-regulation and forms of accountability.

It now fell to the Board of Trustees to reconfigure the duties of governance and oversight of management. The idea of a hands-on Management Committee was scrapped. As already mentioned a full-time Finance Manager, now Finance Director, was appointed and financial control radically improved.

Tim Davis.

In 1997 Sue Atkinson was appointed Senior Administrator (Office Manager as it now is) which strengthened our front of house and daily office management. Already by 1998 the Board had increased a little adding to Tim Davis and Robert Warner, his son-in-law, Avril Burgess OBE, Noreen Nicholson and Monika Shwartz. The latter two had been on the previous management committee. Two years later the Board expanded by the appointment of Sue Glover and Air Commodore Derek Andrews MBE. Tim Davis continued to Chair the Board until 2002. His successor Noreen Nicholson's background was in educational administration, teaching and research. She had joined the Committee in 1992. She strengthened the Board and its

Sue Atkinson

Noreen Nicholson

support for the Director Frank Wood. She oversaw the painstaking review of the Trust's Objects for the Charity Commissioners. It was a sign of a house put in order that the Centre received the Investors in People Award in 2003. She was regarded as an exemplary Chair.

In 2006 Dr Andrew Turton was elected Chair. His term of office continued until the end of 2013, our Centenary Year. In these years the Investors in People Award was reconfirmed, a new Articles of Association were drawn up and adherence to the Public Code of Governance for Voluntary and Private Sector organisations was achieved, indeed surpassed. Reviews of development, marketing and fundraising were initiated and preparations made for the Centenary Celebration in 2013.

The responsibility, function and performance of Trustees of charitable bodies has became subject to a high degree of regulation and monitoring. The old rather minimalist background function has long gone. The Trustees, all unpaid, and in my experience, none claiming expenses, work quite hard. We have five General Meetings a year, and one 'Away Day' or mini 'Think Tank' day, when staff and trustees usually meet jointly. There are other ad hoc working groups, reviews, interviews and a certain amount of public appearance.

Trustees are increasingly recruited by one of the excellent organisations that find such opportunities for people in public sectors, but the internet and other media are always used in addition. Personal connection and recommendation have become a much rarer means. Trustees are chosen after a strict process of interview and pre-

Frank Wood.

interview visit and discussion. The criteria for their selection include two most important ones: ability to deal with a wide range of the issues and responsibilities of a board, and knowledge and expertise in a particular field or fields that are of importance to Centre. For example we always seek to have Trustees who have professional, legal and accountancy skills, and knowledge of the field of local government, then maybe some aspect of public or community health, education and training, youth, mental wellbeing, marketing and fundraising and so on. We conduct regular 'skills audits'. We have to plan for continuity, overlap in service and succession. We are subject to scrutiny by ever more watchful Charity Commissioners, but we can alter our Articles of Association. Within this we try to maintain a democratic and participatory ethos. In any case what remains crucial to the Centre's survival and success will be the quality of its voluntary workers, whether trustees, project workers and supporters, and their dedication to achieve the aims of the Centre in providing a range of health and social care services to the community.

New trustees, some of whom have not had previous experience as trustees, are given individual induction training and a personal Monitor. They may serve for up to nine years with periodic re-election, or a little longer if elected Chair. The Chair is a trustee with experience who is selected by other trustees, and remains as Chair only at the sufferance of the Board. The Chair has no extra privileges or powers, other than delegated by the Board, but is likely to have a considerably greater work-load than most other trustees.

Practice and strategy 2009-2013

The current situation

The Manor Gardens Centre is a multi-functional Centre that provides health and community social care and welfare services. Our objects or aims, which form the most general statement of our mission are those accepted by the Charity Commissioners in 2006 (see Appendix One).

Given the nature of this book as a history of institutional change, it would be inappropriate to dwell too much on a snap shot of what we are doing at the end of our first hundred years. A list of all services and organisations based at the Centre in early 2012 is given in an appendix. For the most part it is business as usual. It is a precarious time for the voluntary sector. We may not be at the highest ever point, but we are far from at our lowest ebb. When times were hard our predecessors used to invoke, with homely wisdom, the old sayings 'If you can't do more, do it better' and 'Don't count your achievements, weigh them'.

It has always been the case that projects come to an end when the need lessens or can be provided for elsewhere. Some end purely because the funding agency has had its central funding cut and therefore needs to ration resources. Research has revealed no examples of a project ending because it was ineffective or mismanaged. Success builds on success. Mental health and wellbeing and training for people with learning difficulties, have long been part of our work, but recently the Centre became involved in the Islington Mental Health Champions Project and this has attracted further funding for the development of this theme in the overall portfolio of work.

Suggestions have been made for extending work in the fields of inter-generational relations and arts therapies. We constantly assess changing needs and ability to meet them. We are increasingly looking for opportunities to form local partnerships with other charities, community groups, education, arts and youth projects. We also wish to play a larger role in influencing public debates within and beyond the borough, on issues of community health and welfare.

We have specific, important lacks that we need to overcome, such as completing accessibility to all areas, re-establishing a viable kitchen function, and a multi-purpose meeting space.

It is our intention to continue to try to achieve a good balance and synergy between those services the Trust directly owns and manages and those of sister organisations which are based at the Centre. These organisations share many of the aims and aspirations of the Trust while usually working in more specialised fields. Most operate within Islington; some have a wider reach. They bring us a significant rental income, and in turn enjoy a number of benefits from their association and partnership with the Centre.

Our 'occasional users' who hire spaces for events, meetings, training and so on, are more numerous still. They are a valuable part of our collective work and domestic economy. Such users do not necessarily reflect the specific interests or views of the Centre but are subject to a working code of ethics.

RENEWAL AND TRANSFORMATION

The Manor Gardens Centre estate

A big factor in our success is ownership of substantial premises. This is despite the cost of maintenance of aging property and the unfortunate perception it can give rise to that the Trust is a better-endowed institution in financial terms than in fact it is.

The freehold of all four main buildings 6-9 Manor Gardens was acquired early on. We started to plan an extension to link the two semi-detached villas. This was opened in 1928. The greater proportion of the cost was borne by the Ministry of Health, but there was a substantial private contribution and a small bank mortgage to help with completion. Almost immediately we began a building fund for further development. The intention was to rebuild the entire block. This would have entailed demolishing the two Victorian villas. It might have provided a more efficient space for the clinics and wards which were the priority at the time. The scheme was abandoned in 1939 with the onset of war.

In the up-beat years after 1980 the building of a hostel for ten young adults with physical disabilities was discussed, but not acted on. The next proposal for a capital building project was in the 1990s when serious consideration was given to building a small block of flats in the car park for commercial letting. This caused some friction on the Board and was voted out. It was about this time that we were listed as a Grade II building of architectural value, which placed some limitations on future developments.

Another moment of high optimism in the early to mid-2000s led to the preparation of architect's plans for a major capital project. This would have rebuilt and extended the Dame Geraldine Hall to which the Pre-School would move, freeing other spaces for alternative use. We received planning permission and building consent for this, but the anticipated difficulty of obtaining the necessary three million pound sum needed in a deteriorating financial climate meant that the scheme was abandoned.

In 2010 we developed the rear of No. 7 to provide a lift and other accessibility benefits. Ideas for the use of a small part of the rear of No. 6 for a new Health Learning Centre, and the rear of Nos. 8-9 have been considered and may be revived.

The site is just under 3,500 square metres with a frontage of about 100 metres by 25 metres. Total room space is just over 1,860 square metres, excluding the rented space at No. 10.

Are we a Community Centre?

We use the term 'community centre' in two rather different ways. One is as a hub of activities that are sometimes delivered or transmitted to a community of users. Another is as a place where people come from a local community, or communities, to participate and receive services.

At the end of the Centre's first century major changes in the dimensions of these arrangements have occurred. The community has increased in geographical extent and has become more likely to be linked by common need or social situation than by a locality with multiple, overlapping ties of culture, neighbourhood and occupation. The connections between the Centre and its members (users, clientele etc.) have become more distantly 'mediated' by telephone networks, internet access to information and advice, and e-mail for communication between groups of people. Compared with earlier days, TV and radio provide forms of social contact and entertainment. So we are currently not so much of a 'drop-in centre' as we used to be. This does not apply to all activities, such as the Pre-School and the Stroke Club. But lunch clubs, youth clubs, clinics and wards are not currently on the agenda.

The Manor Gardens Centre team
The Manor Gardens Centre team consists of several sectors.
1   The Administration
The senior management team is headed by a Chief Executive Officer, Phillip Watson. He joined the Centre in 2009 and immediately began to contribute strongly on all fronts. He had extensive experience in both the voluntary sectors and the NHS. He was CEO of Age Concern, Bexley, Head of Healthcare Professional Relations at Diabetes UK and also worked for Spina Bifida and Hydrocephalus and what is now Carers UK. He was Commissioning Manager with Rotherham Primary Care Trust and Partnership and Planning Manager with Guy's and St Thomas' NHS Foundation Trust.

The team also comprises a Deputy CEO (Christa Moeckli, with special responsibility for Projects) and a Finance Director (William Meghoma), together with Office Administrator Norma Parsad, and their assistants.

2   The Project teams
These consist of the managers of each project recruited specifically for the task. They may have one or more associates, and they rely extensively on Volunteers.

There are bi-monthly meetings of all staff. The managers are responsible for their own reporting, fundraising and accountability. They receive strong support and assistance from, and are overseen by senior management.

3   The Board of Trustees
The current Board has nine members (twelve is the maximum). There is a regular renewal of Trustees who normally serve for up to six years with re-election after three years. The Board elects a Chair from its own number. The Chair may serve a maximum of nine years. The Board meets at least five times a year. Apart from its principal purpose to oversee and take responsibility for the financial probity and well being of the Trust and its reputation, and the maintenance of its charitable aims, the Board is increasingly involved in developing strategy and taking a pro-active role. The Board is responsible for the recruitment and appointment of members of the Senior Management Team.

The Board receives quarterly reports of the Centre's finances, its Projects' activities, tenant activity, a risk register and a report from the CEO on internal and external matters.

Current needs

This book and the Centre's recent Annual Reviews show that the Manor Gardens Centre can deliver a range and volume of much needed services, with highly successful outcomes and at a very high standard of economic efficiency and overall excellence. We are experienced and reliable, co-operative, flexible and adaptable. What we most need in return is, not surprisingly, a steady, reliable and increasing flow of revenue to fund our work. These funds must continue to come from public sector agencies which commission our work, from charitable foundations and increasingly from individuals and businesses who are committed to our aims.

Fortunately there are some useful new initiatives among our potential supporters: corporate responsibility agendas, donor circles, advisory groups on access to philanthropic funding sources and so on. Unfortunately Government policy is far from clear as to the role, value or funding of the Voluntary Sector, especially the smaller and medium sized charities.

The Manor Gardens Welfare Trust hopes to see a revival of interest on the part of individual and corporate donors, whether their primary interest is in a special aspect of the provision of health and welfare services, or in the locality in North London, in the style of the Trust's work, or its historic achievement or its imaginative and flexible forward looking vision.

Members of our present staff. Top left is Phillip Watson, Chief Executive Officer, top right Crista Moeckli, Deputy CEO, bottom left William Meghoma, Finance Director, and bottom right Norma Parsad, Office Manager.

Manor Gardens viewed from the Royal Northern Gardens.

On the right is Islington North Library (1906), and left is the Beaux-Arts building (1911).

PART SEVEN

Review and Reflections

It is possible to read this history in an optimistic fashion, as progress. There is no doubt that almost everywhere you may look there seems to be evidence of advances in health and welfare provision over the course of the twentieth century. Life expectancy, eradication of certain diseases, education, democratic rights and even housing, offer indices of 'improvement', that great Victorian word for progress. On the other hand many old forms of exploitation, violence, intolerance, discrimination and prejudice persist. Some of these are made worse by advances in military and civil technology. I tend to take a moderately optimistic longer-term view of humanity and its creativity as capable of aspiration and adaptability and of making a degree of 'net progress'. The more you examine history the more qualified this stoic optimism becomes. We continue to deceive and trap ourselves in our own social institutions and values. And somewhere there is lurking what for want of a better term I would still call evil.

Despite all best efforts, Islington remains near the bottom of the league tables in terms of social equality and wellbeing. We can all take away our favourite instance of where the Centre has made a measurable difference, some as part of a general effort but often alone or in a pioneering way: reduction of infant mortality, improvement of nutrition, physical health and healthy lifestyles, our work in play and pre-school education, provision of a multi-functional centre for a multi-ethnic society.

Sometimes, however, we may feel as if we are simply stemming the tide, treading water or conducting rescue missions. There has hardly been a year when the annual report has not referred to 'difficulties', 'strenuous effort' and 'struggle'. We have had setbacks, but we have made new initiatives and seized new opportunities. We have adapted to meet not only changing community needs but also harsh realities as to the means of dealing with them creatively and not merely reacting and coping. We might see this perennial process as one of renewal, recovery and transformation.

Services: then and now

We started our century at a time when public health and welfare services were not at all well developed. There was no Ministry of Health. The Borough of Islington had one Medical Officer of Health. This book has shown the complex succession of

134

health authorities that have taken over ever more responsibilities, while leaving much necessary work undone and space for voluntary initiatives. This has affected the type and range of the services we have offered.

Certain diseases have largely been eliminated: rickets, tuberculosis, smallpox, diphtheria, measles, whooping cough and polio. There has been an increase in diseases and conditions of old age and aging: heart and stroke, cancers, dementia, social isolation. There are new medical issues affecting new citizens, whether genetically such as sickle cell anaemia or the culturally determined issue of Female Genital Mutilation, not to mention some resurgence of old diseases that originated in other homelands, e.g. rickets and tuberculosis. And we have health problems exacerbated by modern life styles and behaviours: obesity, poor diet, lack of exercise, poor mental health and wellbeing, sexually transmitted diseases, violent street crime, alcoholism and proscribed drug use.

The Centre has largely ceased to provide clinical functions, while remaining a health service. We no longer administer a range of treatments on site: baby clinics, podiatry, child dentistry, breast feeding advice, supply of cows' milk and other items of health foods and simple medicaments. These are now well provided for elsewhere in other contexts. Sunlight treatment, offered for nearly fifty years, has been generally discontinued. Some aspects of the work at Manor Gardens continue to have more directly therapeutic functions, e.g. the Stroke Club and the Women's Therapy Centre.

We continue to provide for the most disadvantaged and vulnerable members of the community, of all or any age groups, of any religion or none, of any ethnic origin or self-identification. The community is still local in important senses but has extended to the whole borough and some neighbouring areas.

The Centre can make a strong case for being just the kind of institution and service provider that is eminently fit for purpose in the twenty-first century. Dame Geraldine Aves, who had an exceptionally good overview of the larger national and European picture and could base her judgements on many years of experience in the field spoke in these terms in the 1983 public lecture in which she reviewed her life's work:

'Manor Gardens Centre typifies the direction in which health and social services might well be travelling – with its economy of administration, the distribution of financial responsibility, the ease and informality of relationships and referrals, and the absence of any kind of paternalism'.

Style and methods of work: the Manor Gardens Centre spirit
It may be helpful to draw together some of the recurring themes of our spirit, style and method of work.

The first and most often referred to is a bundle of values that our founders and generations after them have found to be what has made us distinctive and popular with 'service users'. The bundle includes human warmth and friendliness, mutual respect and commonsense. It was often contrasted with the more regimented and single-stranded services of public authorities.

The second longest standing value has been independence, part of the overarching value of liberty. As we have seen this has had to be negotiated and concessions have had to be made. In 1943 when the Centre's leadership discussed impending nationalisation, they used the fine phrases 'freedom and audacity' and 'freedom of expression and elasticity of method'. Independence remains as the expression of a degree of freedom of action and pride in a distinctive social institution.

The third and equal value has been the voluntary ethos. This I believe was given a special turn of meaning by its use largely by women to refer to work done by women (by which I do not mean 'women's work' in some old fashioned sense). This was seen as a high moral value in itself. It was also obviously the means to supply the crucial resource other than cash, though that too was often a matter of voluntary, personal contribution. So volunteering merges here with the notion of philanthropy. A small example of volunteering in a more modern sense was the work done by women volunteers from the General Post Office workforce who would come in to help after work and who also raised cash donations.

It seems that after the implementation of the NHS Act of 1948 volunteering was down-valued by government. Since the Wolfenden Report of 1977 on the future of voluntary organisations, volunteering has been notably revalued and is now highly encouraged, alas sometimes as a substitute for necessary public efforts. Volunteers are perhaps more likely nowadays to be people who are afflicted by the same health issues, or have been through similar experiences as those they work with. They are also more likely to have previous training and to receive additional training on and off-site. A considerable number go on courses to upgrade their skills and enter full-time employment in related fields. Within such a multi-ethnic, multi-lingual community there is great need for people who are at home in both the new and old community cultures and can make bridges over into the new, acting as advocates for new citizens.

A fourth set of values concern the kind of interventions we are invited to make in people's life histories of personal health and wellbeing. At one end this involves the priority of prevention. This leads to a prioritisation of dealing with causes rather than symptoms whenever possible.

Training and enabling

These priorities require another key methodology or style of work. We started as a 'School for Mothers'. This sounds a little archaic and even patronising perhaps, except on closer examination. Mothers – especially younger mothers, first-time mothers, mothers with little or no formal education or literacy and mothers from terribly deprived families living in atrocious conditions – these mothers admitted to being ignorant and wanted to learn how to do the best for their babies and young children.

So from the start we have been committed to training and enabling women, and as far as possible fathers, to take care of things themselves and pass the message on. Advice was given, but so too were hands-on demonstration, opportunities for taking classes, and in its current extension not only advice but advocacy and a more active sharing in dealing with multiple issues and gaining access to appropriate external agencies. This methodology is designed to lead to sustainable outcomes.

From the 1920s we regularly had interns or trainees from overseas as well as recommended by the London County Council. School children from neighbouring schools paid shorter visits, sometimes as part of their syllabus. In recent years we have received many students studying for national qualifications, and this is an area of work that is likely to expand.

Holistic approach

Holistic is not a word that appears much in our record and for some it may have a more specialist meaning than I am using here. A holistic approach – seeing things in the round, joined-up and in terms of the whole person – seems to sum up much of our style, purpose and desired outcomes. There are a number of senses in which we might use it.

If we focus on the individual person, then a holistic approach seeks to embrace and combine physical, mental and spiritual aspects of wellbeing. It emphasises the value of integration, centredness and fulfilment. It positively seeks out connections and influences and sees how they have interacted and may be understood and, if appropriate, brought together fruitfully.

An overly individualistic approach may lead to a lack of a holistic perspective at another level. Hence the importance of dealing with infants and parents together with their wider family, siblings, grandparents and other carers. Hence the importance of inter-generational relations and the overcoming of the social isolation of people living alone or with an over-extended carer.

At another level still the family and similar groupings exist in various overlapping communities. Inevitably some forms of social bonding will be provided by the more organic ties of country and language of origin, religion, class or politics. It is a matter of interesting debate as to whether more inclusive and extensive forms of socialisation are just wider dimensions or are something to be desired for their own sake. Thus wider and more inclusive social formations might be built or grow out of relations of locality, culture and other shared values and interests. All this is the greatest importance in current debates about social cohesion and social solidarity.

Partnership

This is a term much used now in new ways within the voluntary sector. By any name partnership with other people and organisations has always been an essential component part of the Centre's work. There is no need to repeat frequent references to our co-operation, partnership with public health authorities or with the three other infant welfare centres in Islington up to about 1948.

REVIEW AND REFLECTIONS

In a sense all our lasting and substantial relations might be called partnerships. Some have been stronger and more enduring than others. Our link with the American Women's Club of London was our most valuable in the period 1916-40. This was overseen by a joint committee that included leading members of the Centre Committee. Also notable has been our link with The King's Fund. At times we have been members, leading members, of various London-wide associations.

In the current political and funding climate there is intense competition for grants and contracts within the charitable sector, from grant giving foundations, commissioning agencies and public authorities. This makes the role of Chief Executive Officer and the senior management team more proactive – and burdensome – and the support of Trustees of greater value. Organisations such as the Manor Gardens Centre have to maintain a high profile. They have to show a record of successful outcomes and delivery of services. They have to be alert and responsive to rapidly changing needs and requirements, and to work closely with the local political authority and health and welfare agencies. In addition to the pragmatic value of such activity, partnerships of this sort have an overarching value as part of our commitment to a participatory and democratic style of work and kind of society.

Problems of longer term planning

Like everyone else we are subject to changes in the financial and political macro-environment. We also have to have regard to the rise and fall of local agencies and initiatives, such as the Primary Care Trust, the Sure Start programme and the new youth and arts facility Platform in Hornsey Road nearby.

It would be an exaggeration to say that we live a hand-to-mouth existence but it is precarious. The Manor Gardens Welfare Trust has no permanent income producing endowment or investments and very modest reserves. Our estate is valuable but its capital value could only be realised in some exceptional, perhaps final emergency scenario. All our contracts (service level agreements) and all our tenancies could terminate without much notice. There is seldom a reliable horizon of more than about two years. It is a constant effort to maintain viability let alone plan for any expansion or increase in quality of our services. Nonetheless, these efforts and our careful assessment and management of risk have meant that we have continued to operate at a reasonable level even in the hardest years. One conclusion from this is that we need to revitalise our traditions of private donation and longer-term commitments to providing general funds for our work.

There is a concern within the voluntary sector that government's desire to devolve responsibilities and funds to the 'Third Sector' will disproportionately favour the larger national organisations. It is our hope, and strongly presented claim, that we are of near optimal size to take on new work in our fields. We have an established record of delivery of services of the highest quality. We are a local 'flagship' and role model. We have the resources of dedicated and experienced staff and volunteers. We own a substantial estate which is constantly being up-dated. We are exemplary in our record of accountability and integrity.

I return to the worrying fact that Islington remains, in relative terms, at the lowest end of a national spectrum of life chances, deprivation and the means to provide greater equality of distribution of health and welfare services. In 2012 it was reported that

'the borough has the second highest level of childhood poverty in the country with 43 per cent of its 37,000 children living below the breadline' (Islington Tribune 13 January 2012).

A large proportion of these live in families with no work. Although infant mortality may be dramatically lower that in 1913, more than 50% of the instances today are reckoned to be due to the poverty of the family. Only the London Borough of Tower Hamlets had a worse record.

At the forefront of our concerns and our planning therefore has to be the issue of poverty: the poverty gap, child poverty, the poverty of the isolated, poverty of the aged and housing poverty. For some social groups even poverty is unevenly distributed, made worse, as a result of forms of social discrimination.

The overriding issue then is that of equality, and equality of wealth and access to resources, not just equality of opportunity. In the absence of greater equality the problems of social discrimination and social cohesion cannot be overcome. Unless this social equality is prioritised and progressively overcome the health and welfare needs of the local community we try to serve will remain unmet. This observation leads to a conclusion that centres such as ours will need to have a stronger voice in public debates and actions on health and welfare and the wider issues and changes in public policy.

I hope this book provides useful insight into the way health and social care delivery has evolved at a local level. And I hope it has done so in a way that we can learn and share lessons applicable to a wider level for the future.

For a hundred years the Manor Gardens Centre has given a voice to, and spoken up for, those in the community most in need. Our challenge and commitment is to continue doing this in the years to come.

APPENDIX ONE

Objects of the Manor Gardens Welfare Trust

1 The Charity is established for the following purposes having regard to equality and diversity amongst, and for the benefit of service users:

2 To relieve the needs arising from financial hardship, sickness, disability and old age:

- to advance education;
- to promote mental and physical good health;
- to provide assistance to children and young people who are in need of care and attention arising from their youth;
- to promote social inclusion by preventing people from becoming socially excluded, relieving the needs of those people who are socially excluded and assisting them to integrate them into society.

The term 'service users' shall mean inhabitants of the London Borough of Islington and neighbouring Boroughs.

Mission Statement of the Manor Gardens Welfare Trust

1 To provide a range of accessible health and welfare services which improve the quality of life of local people.

2 The values that inform our mission and through which we achieve it are:

- a belief that the way basic services are delivered can help to ensure that people remain integrated and participating members of society;
- a commitment to partnership;
- a commitment to accessible services that are equitable and of high quality;
- a pledge to strengthen links with local communities.

Name	Address
No.	

Date of Birth	Children living	Children Dead
Birth Weight	Still Births	Age and cause of Death
Method of Feeding	Miscarriages	

Health of Mother	**Health of Father**
Severe Illnesses	Severe Illnesses
Tuberculosis	Tuberculosis
Teetotaler	Teetotaler
Age at Marriage	Age at Marriage
,, ,, Birth 1st Child	,, ,, Birth 1st Child
,, ,, ,, this Child	,, ,, ,, this Child

Work of Mother	**Work of Father**
Regularity	Regularity
If out, how long	If out, how long
Average Wage	Average Wage
Rent	No. of Rooms
Floor	No. of Occupants

Home Conditions

Measles	Scarlet Fever
Whooping Cough	Chicken Pox
Other Illnesses	Diphtheria

GENERAL OBSERVATIONS.

NORTH ISLINGTON MATERNITY CENTRE.

THE COUNTESS ATTLEE.

CHERRY COTTAGE,
PRESTWOOD,
GREAT MISSENDEN,
BUCKS.

STATION } G^t MISSENDEN 2476.

January 8th 1958

My dear Domini

I am so glad that you can come to see us on Thursday January 9th. at about 3.30 p.m. I enclose the route for your chauffeur it is really very simple. I do hope that Clem will be able to help you with his advice.

Yours are affect^ly.

V.

Left: A Registration form c. 1916.

Above: A letter from Violet Attlee to Domini Crosfield, 8 January 1958.

17ᴬ Thurloe Place,
S.W.7.

Kensington 5713.

1st June, 1961

Dear Lady Crosfield,

We are very sorry not to be able to
accept your kind invitation to be guests
at the Lawn Tennis Exhibition Games on
Tuesday, June 20th, but we will both be
away; my husband in Panama and I in
Russia.

We are so disappointed that we seem
to have to miss this occasion year after
year. We do hope to be free to come
one day.

Very sincerely Margot

Margot Fonteyn de Arias

Letter from Margot Fonteyn to Domini Crosfield, 1 June 1961.

Principal office holders

Patron
1916-1923	Princess Christian
1923-2002	The Duchess of York (later HM Queen Elizabeth, then Elizabeth the Queen Mother)

Chairman of Executive Committee
1914-1919	Mrs Turner
1919-1959	Lady Domini Crosfield
1960-1977	Lady Peggy Turner
1977-1981	Dame Geraldine Aves
1981-1985	Mrs Mana Sedgwick JP OBE
1986-1991	Mrs Caroline Osborn
1992-1994	Mr Tim Davis
1994-1997	Mrs Jane Lethbridge

Chair of Board of Trustees (after discontinuation of Executive Committee)
1997-2001	Mr Tim Davis
2002-2006	Mrs Noreen Nicholson
2006-2013	Dr Andrew Turton

Chief Administrator
1913-1917	Mrs Nora Hobhouse (Hon. Secretary)
1913-1937	Mrs Florence Keen OBE "
1940-1951	Mrs Kingsley Curtis "
1951-1977	Mrs Althea Davis MBE "
1979--1988	Mr Brian Earl (Centre Co-ordinator)
1988-1991	Miss Laura MacGillivray (Director)
1991-1995	Miss Teresa Bednall "
1996-1999	Miss Amelia Curwen "
1999-2009	Mr Frank Wood "
2009-	Mr Phillip Watson (Chief Executive Officer)

Trustees (October 2012)
Joe Caluori

Andy Chaplin

Jenny Coombs

Alan Elias

Daniel Glatman

Patricia Hakong (Treasurer)

Anne Jennings

Susan Lacy

Susan O'Connor

Andrew Turton (Chair)

Services and Organisations at the Manor Gardens Centre July 2012

Managed by Manor Gardens Centre:
Community Health Learning Centre
Community Kitchens Project
Friendship Phone Network
Health Advocacy Project
Manor Gardens Pre-School (Nursery)
Mental Health Champions Project
The Stroke Project
Manor Gardens Centre Management Team

Tenant Organisations:
ABD Craft Club
African Health Forum
African Sub Saharan Development Partnership
Age UK
BAOBAB
B2B Somali Arts and Education
Carila
Centre for Psychotherapy & Human Rights
Congolese Association of Elderly People
Congolese Financial Project/African Permanent Education Forum
CUTTINroom
Elthorne Learning Centre
Islington People's Rights
iCope/IAPT (PCT) - (Immediate Access to Psychological Therapies)
Kurdish Children and Youth Centre
Kurdish National Congress
Minority Matters
MTSSP (Mother Tongue & Supplementary Schools Partnership)
Music for the People
North London Group Therapy
Opam
Peru Support Group/Bolivian Info Forum
Pamodzi
Roundabout
Shanti International
Women's Therapy Centre

APPENDIX FIVE

Donors and sponsors 1992-2011

Principal Commissioning agencies and authorities
Islington Borough Council
Islington Neighbourhood Renewal
Islington Regeneration Department
Islington Sure Start
Islington Health Action Zone
Healthy Islington
Islington Primary Care Trust/NHS Islington
Camden and Islington NHS
Camden and Islington Health Action Zone
Camden Primary Care Trust

Select list of donors 1992-2011
Ahmadiya Muslim Jamaat
Arsenal Football Club/ Gunners Foundation
Baring Foundation
BASSAC (opportunities for volunteering)
Beatrice Laing Trust
Bridge House Estates/City Bridge Trust
British Heart Foundation
British Lottery Fund (Awards for All)
British Telecom
Capacity Builders
Central Council for Education & Training in Social Work
Christadelphian Samaritan Fund
City Parochial Foundation/Trust for London
J Anthony Clark Trust
Richard Cloudesley Trust
Comatec UK
Community Investors Development Agency
Cooper Gay Charitable Trust
Coutts Charitable Trust
Cripplegate Foundation
Margaret Cropper Trust
Defence Social Services Association
Disabled Enterprise Training
Dunhill Medical Trust
EC1 New Deal for Communities
Education Action International

Esmee Fairbairn Charitable Trust
European Social Fund
Family Mosaic
Finsbury Park Single Regeneration Budget
FSA Environmental Health
Future Jobs Fund
Garfield Weston Foundation
Handicapped Children Aid Committee
Charles Hayward Trust
Headley Foundation
Healthy Living Centre, New Opportunities Fund
Heart Research UK
Help the Aged
Helping Hackney Health
Holloway Fire Station
Home Office Challenge Fund
Hospital Saturday Fund
HSA Charitable Trust
HSBC/Midland Bank
Albert Hunt Trust
Hyde Charitable Trust
Inman Charity Trustees Ltd
King's Fund
Learning and Skills Council
London Arts Board
London Boroughs Association
London Development Agency
London Sustainability Exchange
Lord Leverhulme Charitable Trust
Lloyds TSB Foundation
Lloyds Register
London Stock Exchange
JJ Moons
Morris Charitable Trust
Mrs FB Laurance Charitable Trust
NCVCCO
North London Waste Authority
Nuffield Foundation/Nuffield Phoenix Fund
Oakdale Trust
Payne Hickes Beach
Plain English Kitchen Design Company
Prince's Trust
Queen's Jubilee Trust
Rank Foundation
Saint Saskis Charitable Trust

St Luke's Parochial Trust
Douglas Scarff Trust
Henry Smith Charity
Sydney Black Charitable Trust
Bailey Thomas Charitable Trust
Sir Jules Thorn Charitable Trust
Three Oaks Charitable Trust
Tesco Charity
Tomkins plc
Volunteering England
Waite Foundation
Irene Watson Neighbourhood Office
Work Direction UK-ESF/LDA
Matthew Wrighton Charitable Trust

Other institutional donors over the years

Schools and Colleges
Channing School
Grafton Primary School
Highgate School
North London Collegiate School
The Northern Polytechnic (London Metropolitan University)

Media
BBC Children in Need, Comic Relief, Help a London Child.
Capital Radio, Help a London Child
Carlton TV
The Economist
Radio London
Thames TV, Telethon

City of London Livery Companies
Basketmakers
Butchers
Clothworkers
Goldsmiths
Grocers
Leatherworkers
Mercers
Pewterers
Sadlers
Skinners

SOURCES AND SELECT BIBLIOGRAPHY

Archival materials
Manor Gardens Centre, 6-9 Manor Gardens, London N7 6LA
Dame Geraldine Aves papers
Annual Reports 2000-
Committee Minutes 2000-
Photographic material
University of the Third Age reports and accompanying documents 2006 and 2010
Interviews - sound recordings

London Metropolitan Archives
40 Northampton Road, Clerkenwell, London EC1R 0HB
Manor Gardens Centre collection reference: LMA/4314
[Stored in rigid boxes containing tied bundles or folders of documents]

01/001-68 [1918-2002]	Committees & meetings
02/007-31 [1913-58]	Miscellaneous
03/001-09 [1949-54]	Holiday scheme
04/001-91 [1913-2000]	Annual Reports
05/001-13 [1913-91]	Press cuttings etc.
06/001-004 [1936-90]	Finance
07/001-38 [1919-90]	Photographs & drawings
08/001-008 [1917-90]	Printing blocks
09/001 [1997]	Plans

Wellcome Library, Medical Archives and Manuscripts 1600-1945
(see under Islington London Borough: local history collections, and Highgate Literary and
Scientific Institution: Health; archives of The Peckham Experiment, The Mothercraft Training
Society and others)

Islington Local History Centre
MOH reports for parish and borough (see Dr A.E. Harris (1891-1921), Dr Clark Trotter (1921-41,
Dr Victor Freeman 1941-64); Domini Crosfield presentation volume; Press cuttings;
Miscellaneous documents

Secondary sources
Anon. 'The Mothercraft Training Society'. *The British Journal of Nursing*. April 1927, pp. 86-7. (1927)
Aves, Geraldine. *The voluntary worker in the social services*. London: Bedford Square Press/Allen
  & Unwin (1969)
Aves, Geraldine. *Pivot: report of a working party on the National Association of Voluntary Help
  Organisers (AVHO)*. Berkhamsted: the Volunteer Centre (1978).
Aves, Geraldine, *1924-1983 Commentary by a social servant*. Eileen Younghusband Lecture (1983).
Blundell, Louise. *A North London childhood 1910-1924*. London: Islington Central Library (1985).
Booth, Charles. *Life and labour of the people in London*. London: Macmillan (1902).
Brelland, Kay. *The street*. London: Harper (2011).
Briggs, Asa and A. Macartney. *Toynbee Hall: the first hundred years*. London: Routledge & Kegan
  Paul (1984).
Buntin, Evelyn, Dora Buntin, Annie Barnes and Blanche Gardiner. *A school for mothers*. London:
  H. Marshall (1907).
Cherry, Bridget and Nikolaus Pevsner. *London 4 North* (The buildings of England series)
  Harmondsworth: Penguin Books (1998).
Comerford, John. *Health the unknown: the story of the Peckham experiment*. London: Hamish
  Hamilton (1947).

SOURCES AND BIBLIOGRAPHY

Cosh, Mary. *A history of Islington*. London: Historical Publications (2005).

Croot, Patricia. 'Islington' in Baker, T.P.T. ed. *The Victoria history of the County of Middlesex* Vol. VIII. Oxford: Oxford University Press (1962).

Crosfield, Domini. *Dances of Greece*. New York: Chanticleer Press (1948).

Crossman, Richard. 'The role of the volunteer in the modern social service.' In A. Halsey (ed.) *Traditions of Social Policy* (1976).

Davin, Anna. 'Imperialism and motherhood'. in *History Workshop* No. 5 pp. 9-65 (1978).

Fraser, Derek. *The evolution of the British welfare state*. London: Macmillan (1973).

Freeman, M. 'Educational settlements'. In *The Encyclopaedia of Informal Education*. www.infed.org/association/educational-settlements.htm (2004)

Horn, Pamela. *Women in the 1920s*. London: Alan Sutton (1995).

Huddleston, Trevor. *Naught for your comfort*. New York: Doubleday (1956).

Humphries, Steve and Pamela Gordon. *A labour of love: the experience of parenthood in Britain 1900-1950*. London: Sidgwick and Jackson (1993).

Jewesbury, Eric. *The Royal Northern Hospital 1856-1956: the story of a hundred years' work in North London*. London: Lewis (1956).

Johnson, B. *The evacuees*. London: Gollancz (1968).

Lane-Claypon, Janet. *The child welfare movement*. London: Bell (1920).

Lewis, Jane. *The politics of motherhood: child and maternal welfare in England, 1900-1939*. London: Croom Helm (1980).

Massie, Linda. '*Women, philanthropy and the infant welfare movement: a study of the North Islington Maternity Centre and School for Mothers*'. London: Royal Holloway College, University of London, MA thesis (1994).

National Council of Social Services. *The future of voluntary organisations: NCCS comments on the Wolfenden Report*. London: NCCS (1978).

Pearse, Innes and Lucy Crocker. *The Peckham experiment: a study in the living structure of society*. London Allen and Unwin (1943).

Prochaska, Frank. *Women and philanthropy in nineteenth-century England*. Oxford: Clarendon Press (1980).

Prochaska, Frank. *The voluntary impulse: philanthropy in modern Britain*. London: Faber and Faber (1988).

Prochaska, Frank. *Royal bounty: the rise of a welfare monarchy*. Yale University Press (1995).

Pugh, Mark. *Women and the women's movement 1914-59*. Basingstoke: Macmillan (1992).

Reeves, Maud Pember. '*Round about a pound a week*'. [reprint of 'Family life on a pound a week' *Fabian Tracts No. 162* (Fabian Women's Group No. 2)]. London: Persephone (2008).

Richardson, John. *Islington past*. London: Historical Publications (2000 rev. edn).

Rinsler, Albert. *An illustrated history of the Royal Northern Hospital 1856-1992*. London: Albert Rinsler (2007).

Rowntree, Daniel Seebohm. *Poverty: a study of town life* [York]. London: Macmillan (1902 2nd edn).

Smith, M.K. 'University and social settlements, and social action centres'. In *The Encyclopaedia of Informal Education*. www.infed.org/association/b-sett. htm (1999)

White, Jerry. *The worst street in north London: Campbell Bunk, Islington between the wars*. London: Routledge and Kegan Paul (1986).

Willmott, Phyllis. *Under one roof*. London: Manor Gardens Centre (1988).

Willmott, Phyllis. *A singular woman: the life of Geraldine Aves 1898-1986*. London: Whiting & Birch (1992).

Wolfenden Committee. *The future of voluntary organisations*. London: Croom Helm (1978).

Maps

A plan of the Parish of St. Mary Islington (nd, but ca 1850).

Gospel Oak 1912. Old Ordnance Survey Maps, London, Sheet 28. London; The Godfrey Edition.

Upper Holloway 1914. Old Ordnance Survey Maps. London, Sheet 29. London: The Godfrey Edition.

INDEX

Index of personal names

INDEX

INDEX